EUGENIA

Lorae Parry

New Zealand Playscripts
GENERAL EDITOR: JOHN THOMSON

Eugenia

Lorae Parry

Victoria University Press

VICTORIA UNIVERSITY PRESS
Victoria University of Wellington
PO Box 600 Wellington

in association with
THE WOMEN'S PLAY PRESS
PO Box 9318, Te Aro, Wellington

© Lorae Parry 1996

ISBN 0 86473 304 6

First published 1996
Reprinted 1999

Please note that revisions have been made to this script since first
publication. Permission to perform the play must be obtained
from PLAYMARKET, who will provide updated inserts for
theatrical performance. The publishers acknowledge the assistance
and advice of PLAYMARKET, PO Box 9767, Courtenay Place, Wellington,
which was established in 1973 to provide services for
New Zealand playwrights.

Published with the assistance of a grant from

ARTS COUNCIL OF NEW ZEALAND *TOI AOTEAROA*

Printed by GP Print, Wellington

First Performance

Eugenia was first performed at Taki Rua Theatre, Wellington, on 19 January 1996, with the following cast:

EUGENIA/GEORGINA	Madeline McNamara
VIOLET/IRIS	Lorae Parry
MRS BASSANI/LILY	Geraldine Brophy
VINCENT/COOPER	Edward Campbell
RUBY/VIC	Larissa Matheson
FINN/PUB JOE/ WALLACE/MURRAY	Jed Brophy

Director & Dramaturg	Cathy Downes
Set Design	John Parker
Lighting Design	Helen Todd

Playwright's Note

In writing *Eugenia*, I have created a fiction, yet the play has been inspired by the lives of several women, throughout history and in the present day; women who have crossed the lines of gender and who have lived and loved as men.

For many women it was the only way in which they could live their truth, particularly in earlier times, when there was little or no subculture to acknowledge or support a diversity of sexual orientation. For these women, it was a way of entering, undercover, a world of privilege, and yet the price of discovery was extremely high. They were often regarded with fear and suspicion. They were Freud's 'phallic female' with no fixed identity; untameable, uncontrollable. Many paid a high price for living in the only way that was acceptable to them.

This play does not purport to be a factual record of real events or real people. For purposes of dramatisation, characters have been created, names have been changed and incidents have been devised or altered.

Acknowledgements

Special thanks to Cathy Downes, whose vision and dramaturgical skills were invaluable to the structure and fluidity of the script.
Thanks also to Susan Wilson, Gill Boddy, Rosa Iovine, Jean Betts, Playmarket, Jill Livestre, Robyn Sivewright and Jill Hannah. And to all the members of the original cast.

I would like to acknowledge the inspiration of Suzanne Falkiner's book *Eugenia—A Man*, published by Pan Books, and Donna Minkowitz's article on Brandon Teena, 'Love Hurts', which appeared in *Village Voice* in April 1994.

I also wish to acknowledge the support of a Reader's Digest / New Zealand Society of Authors' Fellowship at the Stout Research Centre for the study of New Zealand history, society and culture, at Victoria University of Wellington.

Production Notes

Eugenia is set in two time-frames: 1916 and the present. Because the six actors are required to play fourteen characters, it is preferable, for reasons of clarity, to have only one costume for each character. Some of the costume changes require lightning speed from one time-frame to another, so it is also advisable that some basic part of costuming be used in both past and present.

The play works most effectively with a minimum of furniture, which can remain onstage throughout and which can be used in both periods.

The scenes weave fluidly between past and present and occasionally overlap, so in order to keep the action flowing it is also desirable to keep blackouts to an absolute minimum.

The dances that the students perform should have a beautiful and surreal quality to them, as if they are a link between the two worlds.

The contents of Eugenia's wooden box should never be revealed to the audience.

Characters

1916   EUGENIA: an Italian woman who lives as a man
the present   GEORGINA MATHESON: a deputy principal

1916   VIOLET DONOVAN: an Irish housekeeper
the present   IRIS ROBINSON: a drama teacher

1916   ROSA BASSANI: an Italian landlady
the present   LILY THOMPSON: a girl student

1916   RUBY BAKER: a Cockney boarder
the present   VICTORIA STEVENS: a girl student

1916   VINCENT DUGGAN: a Cockney, Violet's ex-lover
the present   COOPER: a principal

1916   PUB JOE: a Cockney boarder
            FINN: a brickhill foreman
            WALLACE: a detective
the present   MURRAY: a boy student

Note: Italian dialogue is translated in parentheses.

9

'You see things and say why, but I dream things
that never were and say why not?'
—George Bernard Shaw

Act One

Prologue, 1916

Italian music is heard. The lights come up on Eugenia, Violet, Ruby, Mrs Bassani, Vincent *and* Wallace. *All are dressed in 1916 costume. With the exception of* Eugenia, *they all sing vigorously—the first two verses of an Italian folk song, 'Bella Ciao'.* Vincent *and* Wallace *stand to the side. One or both of the men accompany the song on guitar. While they sing,* Eugenia *removes her women's clothing and hat. Underneath, she is dressed in a man's suit. She exits while the other women continue to sing. The singing stops and the women speak to each other and to the audience. The guitar music continues under the women's dialogue.*

Mrs Bassani: He was the most beautiful woman I ever know. He knew how a woman liked to be treated.

Violet: She was the most romantic man I ever knew.

Mrs Bassani: Che buon amore. (*A good lover.*)

Ruby: He was a right good lover all right.

Violet: He wouldn't be telling a woman to do anything. He'd ask.

Mrs Bassani: He was bella. Così bella.

Ruby: He knew what it felt like to be a woman. An' when it come to kissin', I'd say he'd rate heavenly. Heavenly plus. He wasn't afraid of gettin' his lips wet.

The guitar music stops.

Wallace: He was a very confused young woman. The body was a house divided. A misused mansion. The dwelling that had been designed for the sacred ceremonies of motherhood became a ribald clubhouse for the mock rites of masculinity.

The guitar starts again and they all sing the last two verses of 'Bella Ciao' as the woman dance the tarantella. Mrs Bassani *sweeps up* Eugenia's *discarded garments as they all dance off.*

Scene 1: School Hall, the present

GEORGINA *enters. She is rehearsing a speech of intention for the position of principal.*

GEORGINA: St Benedict's is capable of becoming one of the most progressive independent schools in the country. If I were appointed principal, it would be my priority to restore the excitement of creativity to this establishment. To nurture the individuality and uniqueness of our students. To turn B students into A students, we don't need to wage war on drug abuse and violence. We don't need crisis intervention. We need preventative medicine. We all know that you can cram your head full of facts and figures till you're blue in the face, but you'll forget them all within six weeks of an exam. The challenge is to learn how to learn. We need to understand in ourselves the nature of creative thinking; to impart this to our students; to stimulate their desire and their ability to learn. If I were appointed principal, I would be committed to restoring this school to its former standards of innovation, distinction and academic excellence.

> COOPER *enters just before* GEORGINA *finishes. He claps.*

COOPER: Bravo!

> GEORGINA *is embarrassed to realise that Cooper has been watching her.*

GEORGINA, *good humouredly*: Cooper! How long have you been spying on me, you sod!

COOPER: Hit them with that and you'll have them eating out of your palm. Listen, our new drama teacher has just arrived . . .

> IRIS *enters.*

Ah! Here she is now.

> GEORGINA *turns around to meet* IRIS *and is visibly taken aback.* IRIS *is also somewhat thrown.*

Georgina, this is Iris Robinson, our new drama teacher. And

this is our deputy principal, Georgina Matheson.

There is an awkward pause.

GEORGINA: We've met actually . . .
IRIS: Indeed.
COOPER: Really?

> GEORGINA *extends her hand and the two women shake rather briskly. They both speak at the same time.*

IRIS: Women in Education Conference, '93.
GEORGINA: . . . Education Conference, '93.

> *Pause.* COOPER *looks from one to the other. He senses a slight discomfort and attempts to come to the rescue.*

COOPER: Welcome to St Benedict's, Mrs Robinson.
IRIS: Ms . . .
COOPER: *Ms!* Eludes me every time, that title! Ms, Mrs, Miss, one never knows what to call you girls these days.
IRIS, *smiling*: Call me Iris. It's less frightening.
COOPER: I loved the operetta you did at St Anne's! It was brilliant. Funny. Marvellous. Wasn't it, Georgina?

> GEORGINA *attempts a smile and a nod.*

IRIS: Goodness, it's overwhelming. All true of course.
GEORGINA: You'll find our hall rather humble by comparison.
IRIS: No, no. Not at all! It's great. Good lights, stage, acoustics. Eerie though, isn't it.
GEORGINA: Haunted.
COOPER: Totally haunted.
GEORGINA: With the ghosts of the past.
COOPER: The kids love to hate it.
GEORGINA: There's a few tough nuts who'll give you a run for your money.
COOPER: There's what's referred to as 'the rough element' amongst the seventh formers. Drama's the only way to knock them into shape sometimes.
GEORGINA: They adore acting. As you can see, they've taken over the entire hall.
IRIS: Great! We can use all this stuff.

IRIS *looks at the furniture: a table and an old wire bed.*

COOPER: You have absolute carte blanche, by the way. Whatever
   you like.

IRIS: Wonderful! Because I've had this idea floating around in my
   brain. It's the school's centenary, isn't it? What do you think
   of doing a play about a woman who lived a hundred years
   ago? I thought I could write something with the students.

COOPER: I like it.

IRIS: Excellent.

COOPER: Just bung something in writing, so the Board can give it
   their blessing. Got to rush! A principal's life is a pain in the
   butt. *He smiles at* GEORGINA. As you'll soon find out, my
   dear. *To* IRIS: I'll leave you in Georgina's capable hands.

   COOPER *exits. There is an awkward pause.* GEORGINA *and*
   IRIS *both talk at once.*

IRIS: I've done some research . . .

GEORGINA: Well, let me know if . . .

   Pause.

   Iris Robinson. Nelson. I hadn't put two and two together.

IRIS: Neither had I.

GEORGINA: Well, let me know if you need anything, Ms Robinson.

   GEORGINA *starts to leave.* IRIS *digs in her bag for a book.*

IRIS, *calling after* GEORGINA: I've done some research. I've come
   across this amazing woman, Italian immigrant, who came to
   Wellington at the beginning of this century. It's a fantastic
   story. Has all the elements: crime, passion, questions of
   sexuality . . .

GEORGINA: Sexuality? Do you think that's fitting? It's a bit of a hot
   topic at the moment.

IRIS: Great resonance for today's schools.

GEORGINA: Certainly challenging.

   IRIS *hands the book to* GEORGINA. GEORGINA *looks at the
   picture of* EUGENIA *on the inside of the book.*

IRIS: What do you think of her?

GEORGINA: Her? *She is obviously a little shocked.* She's . . . a
   man . . .
IRIS: Exactly.

> GEORGINA *hands the book back to* IRIS *and exits.* IRIS
> *breathes a sigh of relief.* LILY *enters. She wears glasses and
> looks unconfident. She takes* IRIS *unawares.*

LILY: Miss Matheson said you were directing the school play. And,
   like, I'm really really interested in plays, because in the house
   plays last year, I was nominated best man. We did this really
   really modern version of the nativity and I played Joseph
   and Mary's mechanic. And he was, like, quite a greaser and a
   bit of a dag and, like, really, really funny! And so I thought,
   if you wanted me to, I could audition for you? Only not
   right this second, 'cause I haven't really got anything prepared.
   Only I could do it right this second, but it'd be better if, you
   know, if I went away and practised something and then
   presented it. But if you wanted me to, I could sing something
   off the top of my head! 'Cause I like singing. If you wanted
   me to, I could sing, 'How Great Thou Art'!

> IRIS *is about to say something, but can't get a word in.*

Or 'The Lord's My Shepherd' in Latin! Which one?

> LILY *and* IRIS *stay on during the following scene.*

Scene 2: A Brickworks Factory, 1916

*EUGENIA enters. She is dressed in a 1916 man's suit and hat. She looks
confident and cocky, as she arrives for an interview. FINN enters, wiping
his hands on his trousers. EUGENIA extends her hand to FINN.*

EUGENIA: Jack Martelli.

> *They shake hands.*

FINN: Well, Jack, what makes you think you can work a decent
   brick? You're a bit on the slight side. Ever worked on a
   brickhill before?
EUGENIA: No.

FINN: You won't know what's hit you. You get shite all over you.

EUGENIA: I am not afraid of hard work!

FINN: Yeah, but have you ever got your hands dirty? The boss expects a decent quota.

EUGENIA: I worked on a very big farm. A long time. And I drive six dangerous horses, down the West Coast. I was the best horseman they ever had.

FINN: We need men with muscles in this neck of the woods. *He starts to leave.*

EUGENIA, *calling after him*: You must not be fooled! I am stronger than I look. Very much strength!

FINN: Sorry, lad.

EUGENIA: I can beat any man at arm-wrestling!

FINN, *scoffing*: Then I tell you what, Jack, my lad, if you can beat me at arm-wrestling, you got the job.

EUGENIA: Bene! A contest. Is good. Is good!

FINN, *laughing*: Oh yeah!

> EUGENIA *removes her jacket and rolls up her sleeves. She sings a line or two of 'Bella Ciao' as they arm-wrestle.* EUGENIA *beats him.* FINN *laughs good humouredly.*

FINN: That's a skill to be had, lad! I'll tell you what. I'll put you on a three-day trial. And if you shape up nicely, you got the job on permanent.

EUGENIA, *delighted*: You will not be disappointed. I do a good job for you. Strong muscles, sì!

FINN, *smiling*: Aye, you can put them to work right away. I'll start you on forty-two shillings a week.

EUGENIA: You will be very pleased. I tell you what I do, I do the best job for you. I am the best man you ever had. Is good. Is very much good!

FINN, *chuckling*: I'll never judge a penny dreadful by its cover again!

> FINN *slaps* EUGENIA *on the back and they walk out.* EUGENIA *sings as she leaves.*

Scene 3: School Hall, the present

VIC *enters. She is tough and cheeky-looking. She reads from a script in her hand.* IRIS *and* LILY *sit watching.*

VIC: 'He was a very confused young woman. The body was a house divided. A misused mansion. The dwelling that had been designed for the sacred ceremonies of motherhood became a ribald clubhouse for the mock rites of masculinity.' *She stops reading.* This is crap. Who wrote it?

IRIS: It's a direct transcript, from the court case.

VIC: Well, it sucks.

IRIS: You think you can do better?

VIC: I reckon.

IRIS: Convince me.

VIC: I don't have to prove myself to you!

IRIS: You ever done any writing?

VIC: Yeah. On the dunny walls.

IRIS: Okay then, so what do you think?

> *Pause.*

VIC: I think I can string a sentence together.

IRIS: Good. So what would you write about this woman, Victoria?

VIC: Vic!

IRIS: Vic.

> MURRAY *enters. He is confident and cool-looking, in an unkempt way. He carries a photocopied newspaper clipping of* EUGENIA.

MURRAY: Wow, she's far out. Radical as!

IRIS: Hi, Murray.

LILY: I think she's really creepy.

MURRAY: No way, man, she is hot!

LILY, *looking at the clipping*: She looks like she shaves.

MURRAY: Yeah, she's altered as. The wonder boychick from hell!

LILY: That sort of thing wouldn't happen today.

VIC: Oh, dark ages, Thompson. When did you arrive on the planet!

MURRAY: Get a life, Thompson.

LILY: My parents won't let me be in it if they know what it's about.

IRIS: Why not, Lily?

VIC: They say the Lord's Prayer ten times a day. And the Ten Commandments twenty times a night! *Ms* Robinson.

IRIS: Iris.

> *Pause.*

VIC: Iris.

LILY, *smiling*: Iris. I think we should do a musical about Kate Sheppard.

MURRAY: Oh bor-ing!

VIC: At least Eugenia was doing something different.

IRIS: Exactly. Lily, it's about other things besides the fact that she dressed as a man. Don't you think?

LILY: Well, as long as I don't have to play her.

IRIS: What would you like to play?

LILY: Ah . . . Are there any policemen or judges?

Scene 4: Courtroom, 1915

EUGENIA *stands in a point of light. The disembodied voice of a judge is heard.*

JUDGE: Eugenia Maria Martelli, you are charged with gross and excessive fraud. You have changed your name and quality to impersonate a member of the opposite sex. You have reversed the order of nature. You have sinned in the eyes of God. However, as this is your first offence, you will be spared the rigours of prison life this time. But if you commit a similar offence in this Borough of Nelson again, you will be incarcerated for a period of six months. The court sees it fit to fine you the sum of ten pounds.

> FINN *enters. The lights come up to full.*

FINN: Ten pounds. That's a fine thing Jack . . . er, Jean, a fine thing, that they didn't put you behind bars.

EUGENIA: Ten pounds! How is it possible. Is too much. Too much!

FINN: I tell you what, I'll pay it for you.

EUGENIA: No, no, I cannot.

FINN: I'll be sorry to see you leave. Boss reckoned you were one of the best men . . . er, best women . . . I want it back, mind!

EUGENIA: I pay you back. Twice. Double!

FINN: There'll be work going down at the Textile Mill, making uniforms for the soldiers . . .

EUGENIA: I am taking the boat to Wellington, Mr Finn. The wages for a woman are only half that of a man. And if you wear the trousers the world looks different. They say that, 'Whoever the breeches does wear, lives a life as free as air!'

FINN: Aye, but you'll not be free as air if they call you up for the territorials. They're talking of bringing in conscription soon. It's one thing being a man, it's another thing being a soldier!

EUGENIA: Me, I like to be a soldier. To fight for my country. Maybe I pass.

FINN: They do medical examinations, man! You'll have a hard time telling them what happened to your whatsit. How would you explain that?

EUGENIA: I would say . . . 'Holy Mother! But, it was there this morning. Maybe I misplaced it!'

FINN, *laughing*: Ah, you're a character. You had me fooled!

EUGENIA, *extending her hand*: You have been good to me.

FINN: I don't know whether to shake your hand or to kiss it, damn it.

EUGENIA: Thank you for the money. You'll be surprised how quick I pay it back. You'll be a rich man!

FINN: Don't let them catch you at it again. They'll not be letting you off so lightly. Don't make your parents disown you.

EUGENIA: My father has already done that, Mr Finn.

Pause. FINN *extends his hand to* EUGENIA *and they shake.*

FINN: Good luck, Jack.

EUGENIA *exits. Italian music wafts in.*

Scene 5: Bassani's Boarding House, 1916

VIOLET *enters with washing from the line. She folds sheets and hums along with the Italian music.* EUGENIA *enters wearing a suit and carrying a suitcase and a mandolin in its case. She stands watching* VIOLET *for a moment before* VIOLET *sees her. The music fades.*

EUGENIA: Signora Bassani?

VIOLET, *slightly taken aback*: She'll not be back till tea time.

EUGENIA: Then is all right if I wait?

VIOLET: As you wish.

> VIOLET *exits*. RUBY *enters*.

EUGENIA: Signora Bassani?

RUBY: Oh that's a laugh, that is. No. She's a much older lady!

EUGENIA: Scusi, scusi. (*Sorry.*)

RUBY: But I wouldn't mind owning this hotel. Be worth a bob or two. Here, where have you come from then?

EUGENIA: Italy. I come from Italy.

RUBY: Ooh, very handsome, Italian men.

EUGENIA: Sì, but the ladies here are far more beautiful.

RUBY: Is that so?

EUGENIA: Sì. And you, you are a very good example. So, if you are not Signora Bassani, who are you? No! Let me guess. You are her very, very young daughter, sì?

RUBY: You ain't half flattering, you Italian thing, you. No, I'm one of Mrs Bassani's lodgers. Room Twenty-One, mine is. On the first floor. My name's Ruby.

> EUGENIA *takes* RUBY'*s hand and kisses it*.

EUGENIA: Ruby. A beautiful name. Ruby. Jack. Jack Martelli.

> VIOLET *enters*.

RUBY: I'm charmed to meet you, Mr Martelli.

VIOLET: Can I help you, Sir?

RUBY, *looking disparagingly at* VIOLET: This is Mr Jack Martelli, a real gentleman. This is one of our servants.

VIOLET: I'm the housekeeper, Mr Martelli. And I attempt to keep a decent house, although that is not always possible. *She shoots a haughty look at* RUBY.

EUGENIA: I am looking for lodgings. And work, if you have it.

VIOLET: You'll have to talk to Mrs Bassani about that.

EUGENIA: Signora Bassani has beautiful girls working for her.

RUBY: Ooh, you are charming!

EUGENIA: But maybe she needs some men, sì?

RUBY: Mr Martelli's from Italy.

EUGENIA: Sì, Massalubrense. In the south of Italy. Is a long, long sea voyage to come here. Many, many months. Is good to be on dry land once more.

RUBY: So you're new to Wellington then?

EUGENIA: Sì. Only a few hours.

VIOLET: Now, I'm finding that a peculiar thing, Mr Martelli, that you've just arrived. Because, you see, we usually know when the big steamships are coming in, on account of Mrs Bassani keeping a boarding establishment.

EUGENIA: Ah! So you are clever, as well as beautiful.

VIOLET: I don't require flattery, Mr Martelli. So if you don't mind, I've got work to do, and I must be doing it. *She starts to leave.*

EUGENIA: You did not tell me your name?

VIOLET: Violet Donovan.

EUGENIA: Well, Violet. I tell you where I come from this morning. Just for you. I come from across the Cook Strait. And you know what I ask on the way? I ask, where is the best boarding house in Wellington, the very best! And they send me here, to The Parade.

VIOLET: If you don't mind me cutting you off in the prime of your passionate speech, I'll be saying good day to you, Sir.

EUGENIA: Good day, Violet.

> VIOLET *exits.*

MRS BASSANI (*off*): Violetta!

RUBY: I hope I see you around, Jack.

EUGENIA: Sì, on the first floor.

RUBY: Charming.

> MRS BASSANI *enters, carrying a box of vegetables.*

MRS BASSANI: Violetta! We have food to feed the army. Is too busy in the market!

VIOLET, *following her*: There's a gentleman here to see you, Ma'am.

MRS BASSANI, *to* RUBY: Cover yourself up.

EUGENIA: Signora Bassani?

MRS BASSANI: Sì.

EUGENIA: Jack Martelli. I am looking for lodgings. Also some work if you have it.

MRS BASSANI: È italiano? (*Are you Italian?*)

EUGENIA: Sì, io vengo da Massalubrense. (*Yes, I am from Massalubrense.*)

MRS BASSANI: Massalubrense? Lo so, che vengo da Stromboli! (*Massalubrense? I know it. I come from Stromboli.*)

EUGENIA: Stromboli, sì, sì! Fammi aiutarti con la verdura. (*Stromboli, yes, yes! Here, let me help you with the vegetables.*)

EUGENIA *takes the box from her, and puts it down.*

MRS BASSANI: Bene, bene. What sort of work can you do?

EUGENIA: Anything. I can do anything! I work as a useful, a stable hand. I chop the wood, I drive the sulky. Anything you need. You tell me, I do it. Io non ho paura del lavoro, ho una forza come un leone. (*I am not afraid of hard work, and I am as strong as a lion.*)

MRS BASSANI: Bene, bene. E meglio avere un uomo italiano a lavorare. (*It is best to have Italian men working for me.*) Violetta, you see if the English sailors have arrived.

VIOLET *exits.* MRS BASSANI *waves* RUBY *off as well.* RUBY *exits.*

MRS BASSANI: Ah, it is so difficult to find good help these days, Signor Martelli. This war is terrible. Terrible! My son, he is fighting in the Middle East. This is breaking my heart. I did not raise my son to be food for the cannon. Che va meglio per noi? (*What good does it bring us?*) Before the war, this house is always full. Very popular, my house. Now is not so good. My late husband, Enrico, he was a very big man, Anybody drink too much, he throw them out on the street! Now he's gone I have no one special to cook for. I miss my country, Signor Martelli. I am italiano first. I have many, many italiano things, pictures of Stromboli, la musica italiana. (*Italian music.*) And I cook italiano food, always on Sundays. Then my daughter and her husband, they come, they eat with me. Then I eat too much! So I go to church!

EUGENIA, *laughing*: You have a grown-up son and daughter! How is this possible?

MRS BASSANI: Sì, sì. Is true! I look far too young. And you, you are older than you look. I see this in your eyes.

EUGENIA: I have very much experience. Also, I am a very good cook. I cook for you.

MRS BASSANI: No no no! Is a woman's place to cook. When my husband was alive, I used to get up three o'clock in the morning, before he goes fishing, is still dark. I make his breakfast. So is good to have a man to help once more. I can't give you much money, but here you will eat well.

EUGENIA: I am very happy with this, Signora. Very happy. I start for you right away.

MRS BASSANI: No, no, is late. You must eat first. Violetta will show you to your room. Violetta!

EUGENIA: Signora, please, first I help you with the vegetables. Is best. Then I look at the room. Then I have earned my dinner.

> VIOLET *enters.*

MRS BASSANI: Bene. Violetta, please show Signor Martelli to a room. He will be staying.

VIOLET: There'll not be a room free until tomorrow morning, Ma'am. On account of the English sailors.

MRS BASSANI: Sì, sì. Maybe you share a room for one night. Put him in Vincent's room.

VIOLET: Is that to your liking, Mr Martelli?

EUGENIA: Sì, no problem. Grazie. Grazie.

> EUGENIA *picks up the box of vegetables. She looks very pleased with herself. She exits.*

Scene 6: Bedroom, Bassani's Boarding House, 1916

VINCENT *lies on a single bed, smoking.* EUGENIA *enters with her suitcase and mandolin.*

VINCENT: Evening, Squire. Mrs B said you'd be dossing down for the night. Come on in. Spread yourself out.

EUGENIA: Thank you.

VINCENT: The name's Vince. Vince Duggan.

EUGENIA: Jack Martelli.

They shake hands. VIOLET *enters with a pillow, which she puts on the bed.*

VINCENT: And here's Violet! She's the best housekeeper this side of the black stump. Aren't you, Vi?

VIOLET, *ignoring him and addressing* EUGENIA: There'll be a room free for you in the morning, Mr Martelli.

VINCENT, *taking* VIOLET *by the shoulders*: I been looking for you all afternoon, Vi . . .

VIOLET: I am an exceptionally busy woman at the moment, Vincent!

VIOLET *exits.*

EUGENIA: She is an interesting woman . . .

VINCENT: She's a cold fish. An' she don't bite easily.

EUGENIA, *smiling at him*: Maybe she does not like the bait.

Pause.

VINCENT: Mrs B said you were an eye-tie. 'Jack' ain't much of an Italian name.

EUGENIA: My mother, she was an Englishwoman.

VINCENT: Oh yeah? Which part of England she come from?

EUGENIA: In the north. The north of England.

VINCENT: In the north, eh? Whereabouts?

EUGENIA: Ah . . . Kent . . . the region of Kent.

VINCENT, *undressing as he talks*: Interesting that is, Squire, 'cause Kent's in the south.

EUGENIA: I am very tired. I must wake up early. To start work for Mrs Bassani.

VINCENT: Don't mind me. I'll hit the pit soon enough.

> EUGENIA *opens her suitcase and rummages around in it. She gets out a pair of pyjamas and dressing-gown.* VINCENT *takes off his trousers.* EUGENIA *turns around and sees* VINCENT *in his underpants and is slightly taken aback. She looks around the room.*

EUGENIA: Ah, can you tell me . . . where is the lavatory?

VINCENT: Dunny's out the back, Squire.

> EUGENIA *heads off with her pyjamas and dressing-gown.*

Oi, if you're worried about getting undressed in front of me, forget it. You don't have to be modest around here.

EUGENIA: I must use the water closet.

VINCENT: Yeah, right you are then. Hey, watch out for the guard dog. He bites!

VINCENT *chuckles.* EUGENIA *exits.* VINCENT *goes over to Eugenia's suitcase. He opens it and pokes around inside. He takes out a wooden box and tries to open it. It is locked. He looks at it curiously.* EUGENIA *comes back, wearing pyjamas and dressing-gown. She holds her neatly folded clothes. She sees* VINCENT *holding the wooden box and silently takes it back off him.*

VINCENT: Nice out, is it?

EUGENIA: Sì. Very clear!

VINCENT: Full moon tonight, son. The wolves will be howling soon. Hey, how about a nightcap?

VINCENT *takes a bottle of whisky and two glasses from under the bed. He pours.*

EUGENIA: No, thank you.

VINCENT: G'won! Do you good. Get that into you.

EUGENIA, *forcing a laugh*: Too much last night.

VINCENT: Hair of the dog mate.

EUGENIA *takes the glass reluctantly and takes a sip.*

Yeah, we had a few blokes like your lot, down the West Coast, digging for their fortunes. They had gold fever real bad. So, you staying here long?

EUGENIA: As long as there is work, I stay.

VINCENT: Mrs Bassani's not bad for an eye-tie. Except for that food she knocks up, gives me the bloody trots. So what about this war then? Are you enlisting?

EUGENIA: Maybe . . . maybe not . . . And you?

VINCENT: Didn't pass the medicals, mate. Strained heart, bad teeth, terrible blackouts. At least that was what I told them.

EUGENIA: So you lied to them?

VINCENT: Well it'd be a spunkless sort of colonial who'd refuse the Empire's call, now, wouldn't it. No, I wouldn't call it lying exactly. Fact of the matter is, I can't stand the sight of blood. Especially my own. Besides, who wants to live in a trench, eating bully beef and dog biscuits. Here, have another drop.

EUGENIA: No, no thank you.

VINCENT, *pouring it anyway*: G'won! What's wrong with you?

EUGENIA: I said no. All right!

VINCENT: Hey, I was only trying to be friendly. Take it easy, sonny Jim!

> *They both lie down on the single bed.* EUGENIA *turns away from* VINCENT. VINCENT *makes the sound of a dog howling.* EUGENIA *jumps.* VINCENT *chuckles.*

VINCENT: Told you the wolves would be out tonight, Squire. You're a bit jumpy, Jack. It's just the bloody guard dog, mate. He goes mad with the moon!

> EUGENIA *doesn't say anything.* VINCENT *settles down for the night.*

Scene 7: School Hall, the present

IRIS *and* MURRAY *enter. They are finishing a rehearsal.* MURRAY *is playing the part of* VINCENT.

MURRAY (VINCENT): '. . . It's just the bloody guard dog, mate. He goes mad with the moon!'

IRIS: Great. That's great! That's the energy. I mean, this man is an arsehole, okay. But he's a complicated arsehole and he's a charming arsehole, so don't make him a black and white arsehole, okay?

MURRAY, *chuckling*: Okay, man. Hey, I like working with you, eh. It's choice.

IRIS: You're not a bad actor, you know that?

MURRAY: Yeah?

IRIS: Yeah. A little bit on the sloppy side.

MURRAY: Yeah, well. Brilliance takes a little time. A little bit of imagination. As in, mental power.

IRIS: You get into the mind of the character. *That* is the magic.

MURRAY: I really like that dude. She had them, like, major fooled.

Iris: Yeah, she was a bit of a charmer all right.

> *Pause.*

Murray: Some of the guys round school reckon you're queer.
Iris: Yeah? Well, it's no secret.

> Murray *pauses for a second.*

Murray, *quickly*: Hey, that's cool by me, man. I don't mind, whatever you wanna be, that's your number. It's a personal call, man. I'm, like, really cool!
Iris, *smiling ironically*: Thanks. Thanks for that, Murray. I feel much better now, knowing you don't mind.
Murray: Yeah, 'cause, you know, it's your choice, eh.
Iris: Yeah, right. Oh, and it's really, really cool by me that you're straight. You know what I mean?
Murray: . . . Yeah, right . . .
Iris: You *are* straight, aren't you?
Murray: . . . yeah . . .
Iris: Ciao!

> Iris *exits.* Murray *looks after her.*

Murray, *demonstratively*: Yo! What a waste, man!

Scene 8: Back Yard, Bassani's Boarding House, 1916

Eugenia *enters with a pile of wood. An axe leans against a tree stump where she has been chopping wood. She wears trousers with braces over shirtsleeves which are rolled up to the elbows.* Mrs Bassani *enters and erects a clothes-line across the stage.*

Mrs Bassani, *smiling*: Buon giorno. (*Good morning.*)
Eugenia: Buon giorno.

> Eugenia *sits down on the stump of wood and pulls out some tobacco and papers. She watches* Mrs Bassani *with pleasure.* Mrs Bassani *comes over to her.*

Mrs Bassani: I like to do that for you.

Mrs Bassani *takes the tobacco off* Eugenia. *She starts to roll it.*

I used to love the smell of my husband's tobacco. He used to say I roll the tightest cigarette. I put the tobacco in the paper and I roll. Then, I lick. Then I put it in the lips . . . *She puts the cigarette in* Eugenia'*s mouth in a sensual fashion.* Then I give him the fire . . .

Eugenia *takes a puff and slowly blows out the smoke.* Mrs Bassani *laughs.* Violet *enters with a clothes basket.*

Ah, Violetta, the laundry.

Mrs Bassani *exits.* Violet *starts hanging out the washing. She is very aware of* Eugenia. Eugenia *starts chopping the wood, putting as much of a macho swing into her efforts as possible. She occasionally glances over at* Violet *and grins at her.* Violet *looks away. They chop and peg in silence.*

EUGENIA: Finito! The wood for the winter. Now I help you with the wash.

Eugenia *goes over to* Violet *and picks up a garment from the basket.*

VIOLET: Not at all! I'm more than capable of doing it myself. Besides, your hands are awfully messy.

EUGENIA: An idle hand is a naughty hand.

VIOLET: Is that so?

EUGENIA: Sì. A man must keep his hands occupied, otherwise they have a mind of their own.

VIOLET: Ha! I thought you were slightly different there, for a moment, offering to help with the wash.

EUGENIA: I do not like to see a woman work so hard, when a man does nothing. Why so? But I must act like a man sometimes, otherwise you think I am so strange, that I like to hang out the hosiery, sì?

VIOLET: That's the God's truth, Mr Martelli.

EUGENIA: Jack. You call me Jack.

VIOLET: What's your real name, Jack? Because, you see, I don't believe your name is Jack.

EUGENIA: Ah, you are so suspicious.

VIOLET: Now, why should I trust you, when I don't even know your proper name?

EUGENIA: Why not trust?

VIOLET: Because, you know, you don't look like a Jack to me.

EUGENIA: So, what do I look like?

> EUGENIA *strikes a little pose that makes* VIOLET *laugh, despite herself.*

VIOLET: Well, you be looking to me like . . . Giuseppe.

EUGENIA: Giuseppe! But this is my name! But is too difficult for the very clever colonials to pronounce. They make fun of my name. So, Jack, is easy.

VIOLET: Well, I'm not sure I believe you, Mr Martelli.

EUGENIA: Jack.

VIOLET: Jack. Now, you'd be better off stacking the wood in the ricks behind the house and I'd be better off finishing, because today is my half day and I don't want to be wasting another moment of it.

> VIOLET *pushes the clothesline up with a long wooden pole.*

EUGENIA: Maybe you like to come for a ride in the sulky? I must go to the markets for Signora Bassani.

VIOLET: I have a twelve-year-old son and I like to be here when he comes home from school.

EUGENIA: Ah! Then you are married, sì?

> *Pause.*

VIOLET: My husband died of consumption when my son was born.

EUGENIA: That is hard for the boy to have no father, sì?

VIOLET: He's learned to live with it.

EUGENIA: Is hard for you too, I think.

> *Pause.*

VIOLET: My only care now is to make enough money so my son can have a proper education.

EUGENIA: Me, I was a terrible schoolboy, terrible. Always running away. I rather work in my uncle's vineyard. To earn money, to earn my freedom.

VIOLET: Aye, but education is also freedom. Because if you're educated, nobody can be making you do what you don't want to be doing.

EUGENIA: But here, a man can do anything. It is God's own country.

VIOLET: My husband did not find that. In England, we were told that this was the very heaven on earth. That there were high wages and we would all be given land. Good land. So before we knew it, we were packed like so many cattle, in the lower deck. Sailing across to the promised land. And when we arrived, we found the wages were no better than in England and that the land was a swamp. My husband died of disappointment!

Pause.

I don't know what I'm telling you all that for . . .

EUGENIA: Is good to talk.

VIOLET *starts to leave.*

There is a travelling circus coming to town, two weeks time. Maybe your son likes to come. He likes to have fun.

VIOLET: That's a kind offer . . . but it won't be cheap.

EUGENIA: No matter, no matter. I have money.

VIOLET: I'll think about it.

VINCENT *enters. He regards* EUGENIA *suspiciously.*

VINCENT: Mrs Bassani's on the lookout for you, my man. She thought you might have done a runner. Think you better jump to it, Jack!

EUGENIA *looks at him with distaste then exits.* VINCENT *looks after her, speaking within her hearing as she leaves.*

VINCENT: He's the runt of the litter, that one!

VIOLET: Is it necessary to be so sarcastic!

VINCENT: Inviting Billy out, is he? Clever bastard. I wouldn't have put that past him. Oh, that's devious, that is.

VIOLET: You could learn some manners from him if you tried.

VINCENT: Oh yeah? And why isn't he at the front? Have you asked yourself that?

VIOLET: Why aren't you!

> Violet *starts to leave.* Vincent *blocks her exit.*

Vincent: Look, Violet, you know me.

> Vincent *puts his arms around her.* Violet *sinks into it,*
> *almost despite herself.*

What does it take to get back in your good books, eh? You
know what it's like, when a woman comes on to a man. He
can't help himself.

> Violet *pulls away from him.*

Violet: Oh, so it's all now her doing, is it?

Vincent: Of course it's not all her doings. I said that. But you
know Ruby, she's a slut!

Violet: I don't want to listen to your language, Vincent!

Vincent: You said yourself she was a sixpenny strumpet.

Violet: Aye! But my real displeasure is not so much that you did
it. For that I might've forgiven you. It's that you lied.

Vincent: I promise, it won't happen again. I didn't know what
you meant to me, till I lost you.

Violet: Aye, and that is the sad thing, isn't it, Vincent? Because
once you realise, it's just too late! *She rushes out.*

> Vincent *kicks the wooden pole which holds the clothesline*
> *up. The line collapses.*

Scene 9: School Hall, the present

Vic, Lily *and* Murray *are unpegging the washing and putting away*
the washing line. They put the washing in the washing basket that
Violet *has left behind. They have just rehearsed their version of the*
previous scene. Murray *is making fun of his* 'Vincent' *line.*

Murray: Ooh 'I didn't know what you meant to me, till it was
too late!'

Lily: Please don't poke fun at me.

Murray: In your dreams, Lily.

Vic: Chill out, Thompson.

Lily: Anyway, why does she have to touch me, when she says, 'An

idle hand is a naughty hand'?
VIC: She's Italian, okay? She's, like, tactile.
LILY: Yeah, but she doesn't have to do that all the time, does she?
VIC: Perhaps, Thompson, we should look at re-casting your role.
LILY: No. She can touch my arm! I just don't want to be touched
   on the bottom.

        VIC *scoffs.*

MURRAY: Oh, gross as!
VIC: Anyway, it's not 'her' touching you, it's me. And I don't go
   for girls. So don't flatter yourself. Just imagine she's a man.
MURRAY: Yeah, get into the mind of the character. That's the magic!
LILY: But she wasn't a man though, was she!
MURRAY: She was dressed up as one.
VIC: Get into the twentieth century, Lily.
MURRAY: It happens all the time.
VIC: She was just anti, okay.
MURRAY: Go for a cruise down Vivian Street.
LILY, *upset*: Look! All I said was I just didn't want to be touched
   on the bottom!

        LILY *runs out.* VIC *and* MURRAY *exit.*

Scene 10: School Hall, the present

GEORGINA *enters, looking for* IRIS. *She has a copy of* IRIS*'s proposal.*
She puts the proposal down on the table and starts to leave. IRIS *enters.*
There is a tension between them.

GEORGINA: I've approved your proposal.
IRIS: Thank you.

        GEORGINA *starts to leave.*

IRIS, *calling after her*: Georgina. Did you ever find your car keys?
GEORGINA: Yes, thank you.
IRIS: It was almost a great night.
GEORGINA: I'd had far too much to drink.
IRIS: I hadn't.

Pause.

GEORGINA: Well, I trust we can have a professional relationship.

IRIS: Of course.

    COOPER *enters.*

COOPER: I don't know what the hell's going on, but Lily Thompson's out there in the corridor, bawling her eyes out.

IRIS, *concerned*: Excuse me.

    IRIS *rushes out.*

GEORGINA: We were just talking about the play . . .

COOPER: Don't know why you want to do this job! Snotty-nosed kids and a Board breathing down your neck the whole time. If the kids can't cope, you're the poor sod that cops it.

GEORGINA: You won't talk me out of it.

COOPER: Want to know the word on the street? The Trustees loved your speech.

GEORGINA: Serious? What did you hear?

COOPER: You've got them nibbling out of your pretty palm. I'll bet a bob each way they'll be pulling your name out of the principal's hat.

GEORGINA: What did they say?

COOPER: Off the record, I've never seen the chairman so stirred. You've knocked his sanctimonious socks off!

GEORGINA: Fantastic!

COOPER: First lady at the helm.

GEORGINA: Fingers crossed. Oh, I almost forgot. Here's an outline of the play. *She hands him the proposal.*

COOPER: I'll bung it on the agenda.

GEORGINA: Do. *She starts to leave.*

COOPER, *frowning*: Georgina. You approved this?

GEORGINA: Yes.

    GEORGINA *exits.* COOPER *continues to read. There is a lighting change.* COOPER *stays reading during the first line of the following scene, then exits.*

Scene 11: Bassani's Boarding House, 1916

Night.

VIOLET enters carrying a bunch of balloons. She is humming and laughing to herself. MRS BASSANI enters.

MRS BASSANI: Violetta! You are so late. I am worrying about you. You are all right, sì?

VIOLET: Aye, Jack took us to the circus. I had the time of me life. You know, he's awfully funny, underneath it all. He stole these balloons from the clown, while the clown was up on the stage performing. The audience laughed and laughed.

MRS BASSANI: Sì, sì, he knows how to please. He likes the ladies, Violetta. Not like my husband. Enrico never had the eye that wandered. Still, is good for you to enjoy yourself. And Billy too.

VIOLET: I haven't laughed so much in a long time.

MRS BASSANI: Bene, bene. Because today we need some laughter. Because today, Vincent is drinking and drinking and very much too much. I tell him, 'Violetta is free to go out with whoever she pleases.' He is a very jealous man, Violetta. Very much feeling. But inside, a little boy. I know men, Violetta.

EUGENIA enters. MRS BASSANI smiles and speaks to him as she starts to leave.

MRS BASSANI: Ciao, Jack. Come and eat with us tonight. I have made some fresh pasta. Very delicious. Ci vediamo dopo. (*I'll see you later.*)

EUGENIA: Grazie, grazie.

MRS BASSANI exits.

I enjoyed Billy's company.

Pause.

And yours . . .

Pause.

VIOLET: Jack . . . I like you very much, you know . . .

EUGENIA: But?

VIOLET: But I have plans for my future.

EUGENIA: Is no problem, we can be friends!

VIOLET: I don't know if it's possible to be friends with a man.

EUGENIA: Is possible. Tell me your plans.

VIOLET: Well, you see, I've been saving very hard for a while. And I shall be setting myself up in a small business soon. God helping me.

EUGENIA: Then you will leave Signora Bassani?

VIOLET: I have been most fortunate to come across a very comfortable position here. But now it's time for me to leave.

EUGENIA: It is not good for a woman to start a business on her own, without a man to help.

VIOLET: I'm quite capable on my own, Jack.

EUGENIA: Sì. A woman can do twice as much as a man, if she wants to.

VIOLET: You're a strange mix. On the one hand, I'm not capable, on the other hand, I'm better than two men put together.

EUGENIA: I see two sides of the same coin.

VIOLET: Well that must be very perplexing for you.

EUGENIA, *smiling*: No, no, is good.

> *They hold each other's look for a moment.* VINCENT *and* PUB JOE *stagger in. Both are slightly drunk.*

VINCENT: Ah, look who it ain't! Jumping Jack, the Gent from Kent! This is Pub Joe. He's the brother of the bottle, he is. He's had a few in, so he's a bit loose on the old trotters, aren't you, Joe?

PUB JOE: My oath.

VINCENT: Jack has got a lack of humour, Joe, but he's made of manners, aren't you, Jack?

VIOLET: Vincent!

VINCENT: Manners, Violet, from such a manly mug as this, are not to be sniffed at. Speaking of sniffing, I can smell bullshit coming from his bumhole. How would you judge it, Joe?

> PUB JOE *burps loudly.*

Well put, Pub Joe, and very poignant! I couldn't have articulated it better myself. Joe's a man of few words, but when he utters something, he's profound. Profound. He's been taking the pants off the Turks, on the edge of the Suez. Haven't you, Joe? Fighting the heat and the flies and the fleshpots of Cairo. They had to ship him home on account of venereal matters. Galloping knob rot to be precise. Ooh, he suffered. He suffered the slings and arrows of outrageous Egyptian whores.

VIOLET: I am not interested in your inebriated nonsense!

VINCENT: Ooh, not enough niceties for you, darlin'?

>   VINCENT *goes over to* VIOLET *and takes her by the shoulders.*

I've got manners though. You know that, Violet. Didn't I know how to treat you?

EUGENIA: Take your hands off her!

VIOLET: I can stand up for myself, Jack.

VINCENT: Oh hark, hark, the runt does bark!

VIOLET: Vincent!

VINCENT: I don't think a doggie of your dimensions, would have too much to whine about. Do you, Joe?

>   PUB JOE *burps again.*

EUGENIA: Try me.

VINCENT: Ooh, I never turn down a challenge, never 'ave done. A duel at dawn, will it be then?

>   EUGENIA *takes off her jacket and rolls up her sleeves.* VINCENT *follows suit.*

VIOLET: Oh, for heaven's sake! You don't have to parade about for my benefit. Proving what a couple of men you are.

VINCENT: G'won. Place a bet, Violet. Could be your lucky day. Chance to win a few bob!

PUB JOE: Yeah. I'll back the big feller. The other one's got no meat on his bones.

VIOLET: Shut your mouth, Joe!

>   EUGENIA *and* VINCENT *eye each other. They arm-wrestle in earnest.* PUB JOE *urges* VINCENT *on.*

PUB JOE: Vin-cent. Vin-cent. Vin-cent. Vin-cent!

EUGENIA *is seriously challenged and strains with the force of* VINCENT*'s strength.* EUGENIA*'s arm is almost pressed down, but she tightens every muscle in her face and forces* VINCENT*'s arm back up.*

PUB JOE: C'mon Vince. Vince . . .

VINCENT: Shut up, Joe!

With immense effort EUGENIA *defeats* VINCENT.

VINCENT: Ah, you piece of foreign shit! It's only 'cause I had a few in, Vi. He wouldn't have had a show if I was stone cold. What do you think his odds would've been, Joe?

PUB JOE: Poorer than a plastered plug tail.

VIOLET: Oh, you disgust me, all of you! Fighting and drinking and swearing and carrying on!

EUGENIA: Violet.

VIOLET: I've seen enough!

VIOLET *storms out.*

VINCENT: Now see what you've done!

PUB JOE, *grabbing* VINCENT: Come on. I'm as dry as a desert dog.

PUB JOE *exits.*

VINCENT, *to* EUGENIA: You'll keep!

EUGENIA: Bastardo! Questo bastardo! (*Bastard! What a bastard!*)

VINCENT: G'won. Get back to where you come from!

EUGENIA: Tu sei la sporcizia del mondo! Tu non sei degno di pulirmi le scarpe. Via bastardo! Tu sei sporco! Capisci! Sporco! (*You are the dirt of the earth! You don't deserve to blacken my boots. You bastard! You are dirt! Understand! Dirt!*)

VINCENT: Couldn't agree with you more, mate! It's vermin like you that are pulling this country down the plughole! You can't even speak the Queen's bleedin' English. You're vermin! You got that. Vermin!

EUGENIA *spits at* VINCENT. VINCENT *eyeballs* EUGENIA *with hatred.*

Wog!

Scene 12: School Hall, the present

LILY·(VIOLET) *enters, dancing to Italian carnival music. She holds a bunch of balloons. She is dressed in her school uniform, but has a rehearsal skirt on over the top.* VIC (EUGENIA) *enters and dances with* LILY. *She wears trousers and a white shirt.* MURRAY (VINCENT) *enters. He is dressed in a 1916-style suit. There is a dance in which both 'men' vie for* 'VIOLET'*s' attention. They become so intent on their aggression that they forget all about* LILY (VIOLET).

Scene 13: Bedroom, Bassani's Boarding House, 1916

VIOLET *is packing a suitcase.* EUGENIA *enters with a small bunch of red roses.*

EUGENIA: I brought you some roses . . . from the garden.
VIOLET: They're very beautiful.
EUGENIA: Almost as beautiful as you.
VIOLET: Is that a going away present, or is it an apology for the other night?
EUGENIA: I do not like to fight. Is no good.
VIOLET: Well, it wasn't entirely your fault.
EUGENIA: Maybe I come and visit you in your new business.

> *Pause.*

What will you sell, in this shop of yours?
VIOLET: Flowers and penny dreadfuls mainly. Maybe some tobacco. Because, you see, I'm right next to the hospital. And I'm planning on doing a right good business.
EUGENIA: So you will make a lot of sick people very, very happy, sì?
VIOLET: Aye.
EUGENIA: Maybe I come and help you. I give you a hand.
VIOLET: Well . . .
EUGENIA: Or maybe you like to be alone?
VIOLET: The price of freedom is very great to me, Jack. And this is

the first time in my life I've come across it.

Pause.

We Irish are used to others trying to rule us.

Pause.

EUGENIA: I would never want to rule you.

Pause. VIOLET *looks into* EUGENIA's *eyes.*

VIOLET: Aye . . . I don't believe you would.
EUGENIA: So. I come only as a customer. I buy a bag of candy. I say a quick hello and then I go.
VIOLET: I'm not saying that entirely!

Pause. They hold each other's gaze.

You might want to buy some flowers as well.

They both laugh gently. MRS BASSANI *comes in and interrupts them. She brings in a small basket of food.*

MRS BASSANI: For you to eat when you arrive. Cannoli siciliani. I make it fresh this morning. Very delicious.
VIOLET: You shouldn't be putting yourself out for me.
MRS BASSANI: The boy will get hungry. You will get busy. Unpacking. Cleaning. There is no time to cook.
VIOLET: That's exceptionally sweet of you, Mrs Bassani.
MRS BASSANI: Sì. I am very sweet! Rosa. You call me Rosa now.
VIOLET: Rosa. Now that is a particularly beautiful name.
MRS BASSANI: Sì, sì, very beautiful. The house will not be the same without Violetta. Not the same.
VIOLET: We'll not be far away. You will come and visit?
MRS BASSANI: Sì, sì, Newtown, is close.
VIOLET: Aye, to be sure.

Pause.

I was wondering about asking you something. Vincent doesn't know I'm leaving, does he? Because, you see, I don't want to let on.
MRS BASSANI: Never! Never do I tell him anything. Do you see my lips. So tight.

VIOLET: Thank you, Rosa.

EUGENIA: Cinderella's carriage is ready.

MRS BASSANI: Is too bad you're leaving. Too bad for me.

> MRS BASSANI *exits.* EUGENIA *goes to pick up the suitcase.*

VIOLET: I'll take them, Jack.

> VIOLET *takes the suitcase and the roses.*

EUGENIA: Ciao, Violet.

VIOLET: Ciao.

> VIOLET *stops for a second and looks at* EUGENIA, *but doesn't say anything. She exits.* EUGENIA *is left looking slightly forlorn. She gets out her tobacco.* MRS BASSANI *comes back.*

MRS BASSANI: Ah, Jack, you must not be so sad. Violetta, she is a very beautiful woman, but she is not for you. Plenty of ladies are looking for a nice-looking boy like you. Violetta, she does not trust men. Not like me. I trust. I like men. Violetta, she marries a very cruel man. Not like my Enrico. And Vincent! He goes with another woman, then he wants her back. What can you say? You know, when my husband dies, I think I never, never want another man again. I think my life is ended. Finito. But now, why would I say no? If a handsome young man finds me attractive, I am very flattered. Is good. Sometimes, the young man, he likes the older woman. The woman with the . . . experience. How is it possible to be melancholy when you are with me.

> EUGENIA *smiles.*

I tell you what I do. I take you downstairs. I make you some soup, I make you some tortellini, I open a bottle of fine Frascati.

> MRS BASSANI *takes* EUGENIA *by the hand and leads her out.*

EUGENIA: Grazie, grazie.

Scene 14: Bassani's Boarding House, 1916

Night.

VINCENT *and* PUB JOE *come staggering in with* RUBY *on their arms. The two men kiss* RUBY *and pass a bottle of whisky between them. They stifle laughs.*

VINCENT: Get into it, you old tosspot!

PUB JOE: If I'm a tosspot, you're a swill tub.

RUBY: And you're not up to much, in your current condition. Be like docking down with a couple of beached whales!

PUB JOE: She thinks we're full of blubber.

VINCENT: She thinks she's bleedin' Jonah.

RUBY: No chance of me being eaten alive tonight.

> *The three of them laugh uproariously.* MRS BASSANI *comes out in a dressing-gown.*

MRS BASSANI: What is going on here! Making such a noise in the middle of the night. You wake up the dead! Che unbriaconi sieti! (*What a drunken noise!*)

PUB JOE: Sorry, Mrs B.

VINCENT: Apologies, Mrs B. Just a little bit of fun between friends. Would you care to join us?

MRS BASSANI: What do you think this is? A bordello! Go on. Get to bed!

VINCENT: What? Your bed or mine?

> MRS BASSANI *blocks her door.* VINCENT *tries to see in.*

Oops! Pardon me. Didn't realise you had company. Excuse us, per favore.

RUBY: Vince! You're making a nuisance of yourself. I'll tuck them up quietly, Mrs B.

> RUBY *pushes them.*

MRS BASSANI: That man is a drunken fool. I don't know why I have him in this house. Oh my God!

> MRS BASSANI *watches them for a second, tightening her robe around her. As she leaves, she speaks Italian to someone inside her bedroom.*

PUB JOE *and* VINCENT: 'How they laughed and stamped and
    pounded, till the tavern roof resounded, and the host looked
    on astounded, as they drank the bleedin' ale!'
PUB JOE: I'll drink to that.
VINCENT, *imitating* MRS BASSANI: 'What do you think this is? A
    bordello?'
RUBY: Bleedin' not likely!
PUB JOE: Hang on, hang on, didn't you see that look on her kisser?
VINCENT: If you ask me, Mrs B has been exchanging dirty doings
    with one of them English sailors.
PUB JOE: Up on the high seas.
VINCENT: Rollin' in the waves!

> *They all laugh drunkenly and fall onto the bed. They stay
> there during the following scene.*

Scene 15: Violet's Flower Shop, 1916

Early morning.

VIOLET *enters with her suitcase, the basket of cannoli and the roses
that* EUGENIA *gave her. She looks around with delight.* EUGENIA *enters.*
VIOLET *is slightly shocked to see her. Pause.*

EUGENIA: I have come to buy some flowers.
VIOLET: Well, you might've given me time to unpack, this a.m.

> *Pause.*

EUGENIA: I cannot stop thinking of you . . . Do you understand?

> *Pause.*

VIOLET: Yes . . . *She looks slightly distressed.* I don't know what the
    neighbours will think. Having a gentleman calling, the
    morning after we've moved in. The sun is barely over the
    horizon!
EUGENIA: They will think I am a friend. Trust me.
VIOLET, *angrily*: Now why should I trust you! I told you I wanted
    a clean start and you trail after me, the moment I move in!
    Do you not understand it can be frightening for a woman to

be followed? And how do I know that Vincent didn't follow you here as well!

EUGENIA: I did not come straight here. I had a small stop on the way.

VIOLET: Well, I've no flowers for sale, so you can come back next week when we've opened.

EUGENIA: I am not like other men.

Pause. VIOLET *sighs.*

VIOLET: Will you just leave?

EUGENIA: I brought you a gift.

VIOLET: Are you trying to wear me down, Jack Martelli?

EUGENIA: Sì, I'm trying. But I am not doing so good.

Pause.

So I give you the gift anyway. Is no good for me. Is too small.

VIOLET *takes the gift and opens it.*

It is a ring.

VIOLET: Yes, yes, I can see it's a ring.

EUGENIA: Try it on.

VIOLET: Jack . . . it's very beautiful, but what does it say? I belong to you? I don't want to belong to any man. It's not enough.

EUGENIA: Not enough? Then I have some more, just in case.

EUGENIA *produces a string of rings, all tied together.*

VIOLET, *laughing*: Where did you get such a number of rings? That's two months' wages.

EUGENIA: I robbed a jewelery shop.

VIOLET *looks alarmed.*

At gunpoint.

VIOLET *starts to usher* EUGENIA *out.*

VIOLET: Jesus, Mary and Joseph! I don't want anything to be doing with stolen property!

EUGENIA: No, no, no, no, no! From the moment I see you, I begin to save my money.

VIOLET: You're altogether crazy!

EUGENIA: Because I think to myself, one ring is not enough for
    this Violet. She would like a ring for every finger.
VIOLET: But you're very sweet.
EUGENIA: The jeweler did not think so.
VIOLET: And your sense of humour is altogether frightful.
EUGENIA: So, it is a problem for you if I stay, sì?

> *Pause.* VIOLET *looks at* EUGENIA *intensely.*

VIOLET: Sì. My problem would be hiding my desire for you.

> *The two of them look at one another.* EUGENIA *comes over
> to* VIOLET *and stands in front of her. She touches* VIOLET'*s
> face with her fingertips. It is slow and charged and erotic.
> They hold eye contact as* EUGENIA *traces* VIOLET'*s lips. The
> lights fade.*

Scene 16: Bedroom,
Bassani's Boarding House, 1916

VINCENT *and* RUBY *are asleep on the single bed.* PUB JOE *is lying on
the floor by the bed. They wake, all rather hungover.*

VINCENT: Ooh, I've got a mouth like a dung beetle's bum.

> VINCENT *grabs* RUBY.

Come here, you little land-siren.

> VINCENT *puts* RUBY'*s hand on his crotch.*

RUBY: Oh you'd be hopeful. Nothin' will raise your spirits this
    morning.

> PUB JOE *starts foraging around under the bed.*

VINCENT: Ooh, you know how to get a spark up! Tell you what
    Rube, I'm never going to flat an Irish woman again.
RUBY: I've heard that before.
VINCENT: Cross me heart. 'Their mutton and their beef are all
    wild runts, their teeth are all rotten and so are their . . .'

> RUBY *biffs him.*

. . . private portions!

PUB JOE: Here, someone's pinched me mother's milk! Me whisky's not here. Hey! Whose room is this?

VINCENT: It's yours, you stupid berk.

PUB JOE: Can't be mine, I always keep a bottle under me bed.

RUBY: If it's not your bleedin' room, whose is it then?

PUB JOE: I don't know. Some soddin' teetotaller!

RUBY: Aye. And he's out having a cuppa! And I'd sooner clear off, before he comes back!

VINCENT: Well, he hasn't come home all night, has he. So stop your yabbering.

> VINCENT *pulls* RUBY *to him.*

RUBY: Here, what's this then?

> RUBY *rummages under the pillow and produces a gun.*

VINCENT: Bleedin' hell!

PUB JOE: Don't shoot, Ruby! I promise I'll not touch another drop.

VINCENT: Strike a flaming light! Here, gimme that!

RUBY: Ooh, I got an uncanny feeling suddenly. Let's just hop it.

VINCENT: Hey, hang on, hang on! This is the runt's room, that's what this is! Well I'll be buggered. What else have we got here, I do wonder. *He starts searching around under the bed.*

RUBY: Vincent! You can't go rummaging around a person's private possessions. It's against the law!

VINCENT: I'm a law abiding citizen, Ruby.

> VINCENT *pulls out* EUGENIA's *suitcase from under the bed.*

And I'm interested in the course of justice.

PUB JOE: And I'm interested in taking the judge for a walk. Me bobble's fairly bursting. Ooh, I'm as crook as a gum digger's dog.

> PUB JOE *goes out.*

RUBY: Vincent! I'm asking you to leave his things be!

VINCENT: Leave off! I'd just like a little look at this boy's box of toys.

> VINCENT *pushes* RUBY *away, opens the suitcase and produces the box.*

RUBY: Ow! You hurt my mollies, you big brute!

> RUBY *thumps him.*

VINCENT: Ruby, Ruby, give a man a go! I'm trying to find out the truth, that's all. Is there anything wrong with that? You may not think so, but the truth is exceptionally important to me. Exceptionally.

> VINCENT *opens the wooden box.* RUBY *and* VINCENT *stare at its contents in horror.*

Well I never did . . .

RUBY: What is it?

VINCENT: Well it's not a bleedin' candlestick, is it?

RUBY: Oh that's . . . that's disgusting, that is. I couldn't have . . . Oh, Vince . . .

VINCENT, *looking at her and starting to laugh*: Oh Rube, you didn't! Did you?

RUBY: I did!

VINCENT: Then you were taken for a ride, my darling. On a flippin' great gelding!

RUBY: Oh, I couldn't have . . .

VINCENT: No, you couldn't have ground much with this pestle!

RUBY: But . . . he was so nice . . . he was so . . . Ooh, I thought he was too good to be true. Oh I feel sick suddenly. No wonder he kept it up for so long!

> RUBY *exits.* VINCENT *finds another box and opens it.*

VINCENT: Here, what's this? Another one! An' this one's missing. Oh, you little beauty. You deceptive little sugar stick. So that's how he's been ploughing the promised land! Our Violet's going to be tickled pink when she finds out about this. This should take him down a buttonhole lower! That's nice. That's really nice. I can't wait to see her face! *He laughs and exits.*

Scene 17: School Hall, the present

Iris *enters, reading a book and brimming with excitement.* Georgina *enters.*

Georgina: I need to talk to you . . .

Iris: I've just discovered this fantastic book in the library! The letters and poems of Violet Donovan, the woman she married. Listen to this.

Georgina: I need to talk to you. About the subject material.

    Pause.

Iris: Oh?

Georgina: I am in the process of applying for the position of principal. It's a position I have coveted for quite some years. Between you and me, I'm . . . I'm comfortable . . . with the subject matter. But I am anticipating that the Board might not be.

Iris: Not a good role model for private students. Is that what you're saying?

Georgina: I'm saying that I want to avoid embarrassment, by anticipating the Board's next move.

Iris: I didn't think it was their decision.

Georgina: It's not.

Iris: So who's decision is it then?

Georgina: It's mine, but . . .

Iris: But?

Georgina: It's a bit like playing a game of chess.

Iris: And the students are the pawns?

Georgina: Yes. It's very feudal.

Iris: You've never struck me as a very good serving wench.

Georgina: I like to at least make an effort.

Iris: Do you?

Georgina: I'm simply asking you to tone it down a little, that's all. Keep it . . . seemly.

Iris: Well I'm not planning on having them make love on stage, if that's what you're worried about!

Georgina: I should think not.

Iris: I'll keep it clean. Cross my heart.

GEORGINA: Thank you! *She starts to leave.*

IRIS: Are you still married, Georgina?

GEORGINA: Is that relevant?

IRIS: Must be stressful playing chess every day. I was just wondering whether you had any support away from here.

GEORGINA: Divorced.

IRIS: A lack of chemistry?

GEORGINA: And you?

IRIS: I'm gay, remember?

> *Pause.*

GEORGINA: Yes, I know that! I was meaning, do you have a partner?

IRIS: Oh, right, yes. I mean, no! We were both Catholics. Too much mandatory guilt. I'm always attracted to the wrong women.

GEORGINA: Oh, so you're a Catholic?

IRIS: Ex!

GEORGINA: Wasn't Eugenia a Catholic?

IRIS, *starting to laugh*: Yeah. Yeah, she was actually.

GEORGINA: What's so funny?

IRIS: The ultimate guilty Catholic.

GEORGINA: Has it ever occurred to you that she might've been innocent?

IRIS: Put it this way, it took me years to figure out that Catholics don't need to commit a crime in order to be guilty. We just have to think it.

GEORGINA: Can I borrow this book?

> GEORGINA *takes the book out of* IRIS*'s hand, before* IRIS *has a chance to reply. She exits, absorbed in the book.*

IRIS: Sure.

> IRIS *exits.*

Scene 18: School Hall, the present

Night. Dark.

Lily, Vic and Murray come bursting in to the school hall. They carry a variety of stage props and are wearing the costumes they wore in the dance they did earlier. Vic carries a large, free-standing candelabrum.

Lily: I brought the rings.

Murray: I brought the box.

Vic, *positioning the candelabrum*: And I found this in my grandmother's attic. It's for the atmos!

Lily: It's really creepy in here at night.

Murray: Ooh, spook-ee!

Lily: Shouldn't we wait for Ms Robinson? Iris.

Vic: Nah. Let's just get into it. Then we'll have something to show her.

Murray: Hey! I just had a thought. Do you think Ms Robinson keeps a box like this under her bed?

Vic: Oh, Murray!

Lily: Shhh, she might come in and hear you!

Vic: You're lowering the tone, Murray.

Lily: What's that noise?

Murray: Chill, Lil.

Lily: I've just had a shiver down my spine.

Vic: Lily, come and stand by the candles. Murray, you light them.

Murray: On your bike! What did your last Bic Flick die of, Vic? *He laughs uproariously.* Hey that's really funny.

Vic: Murray, you're a dickhead.

> Murray *lights the candles.*

Lily: I want to wait for Iris. I do!

Murray: Ooh, I'll play with you.

Vic: Murray, you're the priest.

Murray: Oh, suck!

Vic, *to* Lily: Thompson . . . Lily, can we just give it a go.

> Vic *kneels in front of* Lily *and hands her a small box.*

So, I give you the box and you say . . .

LILY (VIOLET): What is it?

MURRAY: It's a box of tricks!

VIC (EUGENIA): It's a ring.

LILY: It's sacrilegious for a woman to marry a woman!

MURRAY: Yeah, I reckon a dude should play her! That's really radical.

LILY: The bible says, 'a woman shall not wear that which pertaineth to a man, or risk being an abomination'.

VIC: Just take the bloody ring!

LILY: It doesn't fit!

MURRAY: I'll play your part, Thompson.

VIC, *starting to leave in a huff:* Jesus! What's the point!

LILY: No, Vic! I didn't say I didn't want to play her!

MURRAY: Too late, Thompson.

LILY: Vic please . . . *She starts saying her lines very quickly.* It's a very beautiful ring, Jack. And I can see that it fits, but I just don't know if I'm ready for such a commitment.

> LILY *breaks out of character and addresses* VIC.

I'm sorry . . .

VIC (EUGENIA), *coming back:* Well! *If* you were ready for such a commitment, and *if* you could trust me, just a little! And if you could love a man who would cook for you . . .

> EUGENIA *and* VIOLET *enter, in their own time-frame.*

. . . clean for you, keep your flower shop for you, care for you . . . then tell me . . . do you think you could be my wife?

> VIOLET, EUGENIA *and* LILY *all speak at the same time.*

LILY (VIOLET): I do.

VIOLET: I do.

EUGENIA: I do.

MURRAY (PRIEST): Place the ring on the finger.

> VIC, LILY *and* MURRAY *exit.* EUGENIA *puts the ring on* VIOLET's *finger. They kiss. The lights fade.*

Act Two

Scene 1: Violet's Flower Shop, 1916

EUGENIA *carries* VIOLET *over the threshold.* VIOLET *is carrying a suitcase and* EUGENIA'*s mandolin in a case. They enter laughing.*

VIOLET: Oh, Jack. I'm too heavy for you!
EUGENIA: No. You are light as a feather!

     EUGENIA *puts* VIOLET *down.*

VIOLET: A feather mattress! Ooh, I'm so happy I don't want to go any further. I want to stay right here. Right on this threshold. To have it lying in front of me, looming on the horizon. I want the anticipation to last and last. Oh, Jack. I don't want the domestics and the day-to-day to swallow us. I want us always to recognise each other's . . . newness. Do you understand? And not to tie each other into forever because of the ring. But to be with each other because it's marvellous and not only because we're married. Will you promise me one thing? Will you promise that if we ever stop seeing each other, really seeing, then we'll go our separate ways?
EUGENIA: Not possible. Is not possible that I stop.
VIOLET: Promise.
EUGENIA: Per sempre. Anche quando non ci saremo più. (*Always and forever. Even when we are no longer alive.*)
VIOLET, *sensuously*: Guiseppe . . . 'I like to say your name. I like the lilt of it on my lips. I like the way it slips and slides, as I test and try. I like the way it captures your essence. I like its poem and rhyme. Its cadent candescence, its peak and its prime. And most of all, I like the way I can take it and tone it. Any time of night or day. Your taste on my lips.'

    Pause.

It's a poem. I made it for you.
EUGENIA: Bellissimo.

> EUGENIA *touches* VIOLET.

VIOLET: Ooh, where did you learn to touch a woman the way you do?
EUGENIA: This is my secret, mia bella.
VIOLET: I don't know anything about you, and yet . . . yet when I saw you, I thought as if I'd known you forever.
EUGENIA: Maybe. Maybe in another lifetime.
VIOLET: Do you believe we live again and again, Jack?
EUGENIA: Sì. Is normal. The spirit is old. So old. Older than the trees, the moon, the sands. But this is our time. This. This now.
VIOLET: And I am wanting every delicious, delectable, dirty, moment of it.
EUGENIA: I'll take the light out.
VIOLET: No. I want to see you.
EUGENIA: Wait! I have something for you.

> EUGENIA *takes the mandolin out of its case.*

VIOLET, *laughing*: Oh, Jack, you're such a romantic.
EUGENIA: La musica italiana! (*Italian music!*)

> EUGENIA *sings and plays a verse from 'Bella Ciao' on the mandolin.*
>
> LILY *and* VIC *enter.* VIC *is singing simultaneously with* EUGENIA, *although niether couple is aware of the other.* EUGENIA *and* VIOLET *stay on stage, in their own time-frame.* LILY *and* VIC *are rehearsing. The dialogue in one time-frame picks up from the dialogue in the other time-frame.*

LILY (VIOLET): Where did you learn to sing like that, Jack?
VIC: Sister Mary Leo!

> *They both laugh.*

LILY: Where did we get up to?

> *They look at their scripts.* VIC *and* LILY *stay on stage.*

VIOLET: And why are you so nervous now, might I ask?

EUGENIA: It is because I desire you too much.

VIOLET: Then if I turn out the light will that make you more confident?

EUGENIA: Sì.

VIOLET: Then I'll open the curtains and I'll let the moonlight come creeping in.

> *Lighting change. Moonlight through an open window.*

LILY (VIOLET): Dance with me, Jack.

EUGENIA: I do not know how to dance.

VIOLET: I'll show you.

> EUGENIA *and* VIOLET *begin to waltz slowly. They do not take their eyes off each other. There is a powerful surge of electricity between them. They continue to dance slowly throughout the following.*

VIC (EUGENIA): I would like to dance this dance forever . . .

> LILY *goes momentarily into a trancelike state. It's as though she has perceived a presence in the room, as though she has 'heard'* VIOLET *and repeats what she's said.*

LILY (VIOLET): Then I'll open the curtains and I'll let the moonlight come creeping in . . .

VIC, *looking at* LILY: Thompson, that's not your line.

LILY, *listening*: Shhh . . .

VIC: Why did you say that?

LILY: Say what?

VIC: What you said.

LILY: I dunno. It was weird . . . It just came out of me . . .

VIC: What sort of weird?

LILY: Like, like he sort of . . . wanted me to say it . . .

VIC: Ooh, spook-ee! Maybe you're Violet incarnate. Lily Martelli!

LILY: I don't think I want to play this part anymore!

> LILY *puts the mandolin that* EUGENIA *has been playing back in its case.*

VIC: It is so easy to freak you out. Just get a life.

LILY: Don't say that!

Vic: Say what?
Lily: Get a life!
Vic: Why not?
Lily: Because I've already got one!
Vic: Let's just . . . leave it for today, okay?

>   *Pause.*

Lily: Okay . . .
Vic: Just chill.

>   Lily *nods. Pause.*

Lily: Sorry, sorry . . .

>   *Mandolin music.* Vic *and* Lily *exit.* Eugenia *unbuttons*
>   Violet's *blouse and removes it. She wears a chemise*
>   *underneath. There is passion and urgency between them.*
>   *They kiss as they make their way to the bed.*

Scene 2: Violet's Flower Shop, 1916

Violet *is sleeping. Loose flowers and a basket lie on the table.*

Mrs Bassani *(off)*: Violetta!

>   Violet *wakes and hurriedly puts her shirt on.*

Violetta.

>   Mrs Bassani *enters.*

Violet: Rosa.
Mrs Bassani: Ah! Violetta. Ciao bella. Come stai? (*How are you?*)

>   Violet *is still doing up her blouse.*

So this is the little flower shop! So small, Violetta. Are you
making the money?
Violet: Enough.
Mrs Bassani: It will get better. I bring you something to warm
the house. A bible. I have too many. So you can pray for
more money.

MRS BASSANI *gives* VIOLET *the present.* VIOLET *laughs.*

VIOLET: The business will soon pick up. But you, you're a stranger in these parts.

MRS BASSANI: Because they cannot do without me at the hotel! Now I am the nursemaid, the manager, the madonna. Is crazy. Crazy! So, I am on my way to the church. Is the only place to escape.

VIOLET: Well it's a delight to see you, to be sure.

MRS BASSANI: And you, Violetta. You are happy, as a married woman?

VIOLET: Happy? I confess to not knowing the meaning of the word until now. My husband is too good to be true. He won't let me lift a finger, Rosa. And at night, well, I'd be lying if I didn't say that was the best part. At night he's an angel on earth.

MRS BASSANI: Sì, sì, he was good . . . around the hotel! He is here? I like to congratulate him.

VIOLET: He'll be back soon. He's out doing deliveries.

MRS BASSANI: I have a letter, arrived for him. Italiano name, from the south. Maybe is family.

VIOLET: His family are all dead.

MRS BASSANI: Maybe.

VIOLET: He told me so himself.

MRS BASSANI: I have been around a long time, Violetta. Jack, he is a very private man. Very private. Once, he tells me, he hates his papa. So I say, 'maybe'. Maybe they are only dead in here. *She taps her chest.*

   Pause.

VIOLET: I'll give him the letter.

   MRS BASSANI *gives the letter to* VIOLET. EUGENIA *enters.*

MRS BASSANI: Ah Jack! Jack. We are just talking about you.

   Pause. EUGENIA *looks uneasy for a brief moment.* VIOLET *beams at* EUGENIA.

EUGENIA: Buono. Come stai?

MRS BASSANI: Bene, bene. Violetta is telling me you are an angel

on earth. But this, I already know! She does not need to tell
me.

VIOLET: I'll make some tea.

   VIOLET *exits.*

MRS BASSANI: Is good to see you, Jack.

   MRS BASSANI *goes over to Eugenia and kisses her.*

EUGENIA: I am a married man now, Rosa.

MRS BASSANI: Sì, sì. Many men are married.

   Pause.

EUGENIA: How is the hotel?

MRS BASSANI: Not the same without you. Violetta, she is a lucky
woman. I miss you too much, Jack.

EUGENIA: If I was not married, Rosa, it would be different. You
know this. Sì?

MRS BASSANI: So, you miss me too?

EUGENIA: I do not want Violet to hear.

MRS BASSANI: Vincent is trying to find you. He is saying crazy
things about you, Jack. I am frightened for you.

EUGENIA: What sort of things?

MRS BASSANI: He says you are a liar. You do not tell the truth. He
says Violetta, she should know this.

EUGENIA: Why am I a liar!

MRS BASSANI: Ah! He is mad. Mental. Pazzo! (*Crazy!*)

EUGENIA: Do not tell him anything.

MRS BASSANI: What is there to tell?

EUGENIA: Nothing.

MRS BASSANI: Sometimes it is important to have a secret. Is normal.
I know nothing. Nothing.

   EUGENIA *is looking at her in shock, wondering what, if
   anything, she knows.* VIOLET *enters and sees* EUGENIA *and*
   MRS BASSANI *very close.*

VIOLET: Is everything well? You look pale, Jack.

MRS BASSANI: Sì, buono! I am telling Jack about all the things
that are going on in the hotel. Is crazy. Crazy! But now, I
must go. Because the priest, I don't know why, but I cannot

get him to hold the service for me.

VIOLET: Then you'll not be staying for tea?

MRS BASSANI: I hate to be late in the church. When you walk down the aisle, they all look at your hat! I don't like to make them jealous.

> MRS BASSANI *pins on a very ordinary-looking hat, then kisses* VIOLET.

Ciao, Violetta.

VIOLET: Ciao, Rosa.

MRS BASSANI: Arrivederci, Jack.

EUGENIA: Ciao, Rosa.

> MRS BASSANI *leaves.* EUGENIA *takes off her jacket. Pause.*

VIOLET: What did Rosa say?

EUGENIA: Nothing. She said nothing.

> *Pause.*

VIOLET: She came with a letter for you.

EUGENIA: Letter? What letter?

> EUGENIA *tries to look casual.*

VIOLET: It's from a man in Nelson. His name is Martelli. It's the same name as yours, Jack.

EUGENIA: Sì. An italiano man. I knew him.

VIOLET: How did you know him?

> *Pause.*

Jack?

EUGENIA: . . . I knew him in Massalubrense. Many people in my village are called Martelli. They come to New Zealand. First this family, then that family. Then the whole village. Is normal.

> *Pause.*

VIOLET: But not your family?

> VIOLET *hands* EUGENIA *the letter. Pause.*

Well, you better open it. It might be important.

EUGENIA *opens it reluctantly and pretends to read.*

I know you're not able to read, Jack. That's nothing to be
ashamed of. Here, I'll read it for you.

EUGENIA: No!

VIOLET: I don't understand. Do you not trust me now?

Pause.

Jack, you know you can tell me anything.

EUGENIA, *aggressively*: What is there to tell? Why is there something
to tell suddenly? Something to tell! What?

VIOLET: If there's nothing to tell, then why are you afraid of me
reading the letter?

EUGENIA: I am not afraid!

EUGENIA *throws the letter on the table.*

VIOLET, *taking* EUGENIA *by the shoulders*: Jack, I'm your wife. I
love you so much. It doesn't matter to me what you've done
in your past. I don't care. I am truly happy and nothing can
change that. Nothing on God's earth.

VIOLET *picks up the letter and opens it.* EUGENIA *watches
her in fear. She starts to arrange bunches of flowers.* VIOLET
reads the letter.

VIOLET: It says here that a Mrs Maria Martelli died peacefully in
her sleep on Wednesday. And it tells you that the funeral
will be on Saturday. Who is this lady, Jack?

EUGENIA: What else does it say?

VIOLET: Just the time and the place. Was it someone that you
loved?

EUGENIA, *hardly able to speak*: Sì. The mother . . . the mother of a
family I knew.

Pause.

VIOLET: Why don't you take the rest of the day off? I'll close up
and I'll finish your deliveries for you.

VIOLET *runs her fingers through* EUGENIA'*s hair.*

'That the birds of worry and care fly about your head, this
you cannot change, but that they build nests in your hair,

now that you can prevent.' You're a wonderful man, Jack.

> EUGENIA *touches* VIOLET's *hand for a second before* VIOLET *exits.* EUGENIA *screws up the letter and paces around. She picks up the crumpled page and sits back down. She smoothes it out and starts to cry, smoothing and smoothing out the creases. Her cry is a woman's cry, almost a keening. She stops crying and takes a packet of matches from her pocket. She lights the candle and burns the letter. She takes a jug and a bowl and pours some water into the bowl. She gets out a watch from her pocket and looks at the time. Satisfied that* VIOLET *will be doing deliveries for a while longer, she drops her braces to her sides and removes her shirt and singlet. Underneath are bandages which are wrapped around her breasts. She unwinds them and is naked from the waist up. She washes slowly and languidly in the soft light of the candle.* VIOLET *enters, taking her by surprise.*

VIOLET: I forgot the roses I was to take for Mr . . .

> VIOLET *stops when she sees* EUGENIA's *naked torso. She stares at* EUGENIA *in shock. Her voice is barely audible.*

Oh my God . . .

> EUGENIA *grabs her jacket which she holds in front of her.*

EUGENIA, *excitedly*: Che fai qua! Tu hai detto che uscivi! Che fai qua! (*What are you doing here! You said you were going out!*)
VIOLET: Oh my God . . . Holy mother . . .

> EUGENIA *turns away from her as she puts on her jacket to hide her breasts. She swings back to face* VIOLET.

EUGENIA, *shouting*: Va via, va via per amor di dio! Non voglio che tu mi veda! Non è vero. Va via e lasciami stare! (*Get out, get out, for God sake! I don't want you to see me! It is not true. Get out and leave me alone!*)

> VIOLET *stares incomprehensibly at* EUGENIA. *Her voice is almost a whisper.*

VIOLET: No . . . I don't understand . . .
EUGENIA: Tu hai detto che uscivi! (*You said you were going out!*)

VIOLET: Tell me it's not true . . .

EUGENIA: No . . . no . . . Violet, Violet . . .

VIOLET: I don't understand . . .

EUGENIA: Non è vero, non è vero. (*It's not true.*)

VIOLET: Why?

EUGENIA: Sono un uomo! (*I am a man!*)

VIOLET: Why did you marry me? Why? Why did you do this? Why didn't you tell me? Tell me why!

EUGENIA: If I told you, you would not have married me . . . If I'd told you the truth, would you have married me?

VIOLET: No, I would not have married you! A woman cannot marry another woman! *She starts to laugh, slightly hysterically.* That is entirely ridiculous!

EUGENIA: I am not a woman!

VIOLET, *laughing hysterically*: I've married a woman! Oh, that's funny. That's really funny, Jack. The priest married two women!

> EUGENIA *grabs* VIOLET *by the shoulders to shake her out of it:*

EUGENIA: I am a man! I was born a man! I have two parts. It is just different . . . different . . .

> VIOLET *pushes* EUGENIA *violently from her.*

VIOLET: Who are you?! I don't even know you. You've never told me anything about yourself.

EUGENIA: I will tell you everything. Everything.

VIOLET: I don't know who you are! All you've done is lie to me! Oh my God, oh my God, oh my God . . .

EUGENIA: I am the same. Believe me.

VIOLET: I should never have trusted you. Never! I knew you were too good to be true.

EUGENIA: I am still the person you loved!

VIOLET: I loved a man!

EUGENIA: I am a man!

VIOLET: I hate you! We must get an annulment . . . I hate you!

> VIOLET *tries to run out of the shop.* EUGENIA *grabs her and tries desperately to hold her, to convince her.* VIOLET *struggles wildly to free herself.*

Let go of me!

EUGENIA: I am a man. I am a man. Where it is important, I am a man. How do you think we make love?

VIOLET *cries out and collapses into* EUGENIA.

VIOLET: I don't know . . . I don't know . . .

EUGENIA: I am a man. Believe me.

VIOLET, *crying*: I don't know . . .

EUGENIA: Part of me is a woman and part of me is a man.

VIOLET: I don't know which part to love . . .

EUGENIA, *desperately and quickly*: I am still your husband. I wanted to tell you. I wanted to tell you for so long. But I wanted you to know how good I could treat you, before you found out. Do you believe me? Do you believe me?!

EUGENIA *holds* VIOLET *by the shoulders.*

VIOLET: I don't know. I want to believe you . . .

EUGENIA: I love you as a man loves a woman. You love me as a woman loves a man. Nothing has changed. Only now you can know me. You can know who I am. I know that you love me. Tell me, tell me.

EUGENIA *kisses* VIOLET'*s neck.*

VIOLET: I don't know . . . yes . . .

EUGENIA: You love me . . . tell me . . .

VIOLET: Yes . . . yes . . .

VIOLET, *starts, almost reluctantly, to respond.*

> EUGENIA *walks with her over to a chair, where she guides her down. She undoes her skirt and slips her hand underneath it. She starts to make love to her as she speaks.* VIOLET *becomes subdued and responsive. She utters 'aye' and 'sì' throughout the following.*

EUGENIA: Is different now. I will give you everything. Everything. I know what a woman feels, what a woman wants. We can go on. We can. We can tell each other everything. I tell you everything. You must trust me. Sì, sì bella. Beautiful. Io voglio a te. E tu vuoi me'. (*I want you and you want me.*) I want you. You want me. Sì, sì bella. Bella. Tu sei tanto bella. Tu sei mia moglie, e io sono tuo marito. (*You are so beautiful. You are my wife, and I am your husband.*) Nothing has changed. Only now, now you can know me . . . tu sei bella, tu sei tanto bella. You are so beautiful . . . And you are my wife . . .

Scene 3: School Hall, the present

VIC, MURRAY *and* LILY *enter, holding their scripts.*

MURRAY: She was a pervert!
VIC: She was a radical!
MURRAY: Bullshit. She was a sleaze bucket.
VIC: What's your problem?
MURRAY: I haven't got a problem.
VIC: You write it then!
MURRAY: I just feel sorry for his wife. As far as she was concerned, she was marrying a man.
VIC: She *was* a man!

> EUGENIA *enters.* LILY *sees* EUGENIA *and stares at her in disbelief. Neither* VIC *nor* MURRAY *is aware of* EUGENIA.

EUGENIA, *to* LILY: I am a man. Where it is important, I am a man.

> EUGENIA *exits.* LILY *looks thunderstruck. Pause.*

VIC: Well, let's just do what we've written. Lily, you start. Lily . . .

> *Pause.*

LILY: I . . . I saw him.
VIC: Saw who?
LILY: Him. It was him.
MURRAY: You are truly weird, sister.
VIC: Lily, are you okay?
LILY: He was staring at me.
MURRAY: Oh, mental!
VIC: What did you see?
MURRAY: Freak-o. Let me out of here. You two don't need drugs!

MURRAY *exits.*

LILY: Him. It was him.

VIC, *looking at her in awe*: Eugenia? He showed himself to you! Maybe . . . maybe he's like the ghost in *Hamlet*, Lily. Maybe he's trapped. Stalking the earth.

LILY: We shouldn't be doing this.

VIC, *excited*: Why? Do you think he'll come back? We've got to tell Iris.

LILY: Something awful's going to happen.

VIC: How do you know?

LILY: Because I saw it. I saw it in his eyes!

Scene 4: Violet's Flower Shop, 1916

Night.

VINCENT *and* PUB JOE *burst in.*

VINCENT: Violet! Violet!

VIOLET, *in a dressing-gown, enters.*

VIOLET: What are you doing here!

VINCENT: It's New Year's Eve.

PUB JOE: We thought you might like to come and celebrate.

VINCENT: What are you doing in bed at this hour? I can't for the life of me imagine.

VIOLET: Will you please leave!

VINCENT: Now, Violet. That's no way to treat a fellow who's been looking for you the length and breadth of the capital, now is it!

VIOLET: How did you know where to find me?

VINCENT: Oh, now that would be telling, wouldn't it. But if I said we followed our Madame Bassani to church, you'd know it wasn't because we were wanting communion.

VIOLET: What are you wanting, Vincent?

VINCENT: I'm wanting you, Violet.

VIOLET: I am a married woman now.

VINCENT: Oh, I have my doubts about that.

VIOLET: What are you talking about?

VINCENT: Where is he? If you can call him a he. Where is 'it'?

VIOLET: I don't know what you're talking about! Now will you kindly leave!

> EUGENIA *enters with her braces hanging at her sides.*

VINCENT: Ah! Here he is! The man himself. Howdy, Jack! Or should I call you Jackie?

> PUB JOE *laughs.*

EUGENIA: My wife has asked you to leave.

VINCENT: Your wife! Well I never. Did you hear that, Joe? Jackie has a wife.

PUB JOE: He's a clever cockie, all right.

EUGENIA: If you do not leave, I will get the police.

VINCENT: Oh, we'll leave all right. When I've said what I have to say.

VIOLET: I know my husband is different, Vincent!

VINCENT: Oh, he's different all right!

PUB JOE: Very very different.

VINCENT: Have you asked him to prove his manhood?

VIOLET: I have all the proof I need!

EUGENIA: You are scum! Get out of our house, before I kill you!

VINCENT: Hey, hey, hey! Take it easy. If you got nothing to hide, there's nothing to get all agitati about, is there? We just want to see if your bagpipes can play us a tune. Grab him, Joe!

> EUGENIA *struggles as Joe grabs her from behind pinning her arms behind her back.*

VIOLET: Leave him alone, Vincent!

> VINCENT *pushes* VIOLET *away.*

EUGENIA: Bastard! You bastard, I'll kill you!

PUB JOE: Let's see his bobbles!

VINCENT: Let's unwrap the greasy little garlic-eater and see what he puts in his pants. Hey, don't be so uncooperative, 'Jack'! You've been in conference with a castrato, Violet!

PUB JOE: It's for your own good, son!

VINCENT: If you've got any groceries down there, you won't be ashamed to show them!

> VINCENT *pulls* EUGENIA'*s trousers down, and* VIOLET *catches her breath in shock.*

EUGENIA: No!
VINCENT: You can't catch an oyster with that equipment, Violet.
PUB JOE: He ain't no boy soprano neither.

> VINCENT *pushes* EUGENIA *to the ground. She struggles to pull her trousers up. Silence.*

VIOLET: Get out!

> VINCENT *grabs* VIOLET *by the shoulders. She is in quiet shock.*

VINCENT: Violet, Violet. I only did this for your sake. Taking the wool from your eyes. I'm busting me life up over you. I won't lose you again, Vi!
VIOLET, *low and menacing*: Let go of me.

> VINCENT *lets her go.* VIOLET *exits.*

VINCENT: Come back here. Violet! Come back!
EUGENIA: Bastard!

> EUGENIA *grabs* VINCENT *from behind. They tussle.* VINCENT *gets the better of* EUGENIA *and he and* PUB JOE *kick her ruthlessly on the ground.*

VINCENT: You haven't seen the last of me, you prickless wonder!

> VINCENT *and* PUB JOE *exit.* EUGENIA *picks herself up painfully from the floor.* VIOLET *comes back dressed in her ordinary clothes. She carries* EUGENIA'*s suitcase and jacket. She puts them down and watches* EUGENIA *for a moment. She can hardly speak. Silence.*

VIOLET: I want an annulment.

> EUGENIA *doesn't say anything. She closes her eyes, controlling her emotions.*

Why didn't you tell me the entire truth?

> *Silence.*

Why? Why did you leave me in the lying dark? If you're a woman, why didn't you have the decency to treat me like a woman and not like a perfect imbecile.

EUGENIA: I told you the truth.

VIOLET: You told me a half truth!

EUGENIA: I changed it to be my truth. You cannot know what it is like, to be born in the skin of the wrong sex. To lie is the only way to live my truth. What is a man? Only what the world sees, what we feel inside. What did you love before, that you cannot love now? I am still the same inside.

VIOLET: You even lied to me about your family.

EUGENIA: I have no family! My family have disowned me. And now my mother is dead.

VIOLET: Why didn't you tell me that was your mother?

    Silence.

EUGENIA: Now you know the truth.

VIOLET: The truth? I don't even know where you come from. I don't even know your name!

    Silence.

EUGENIA: My name . . . I have almost forgot. In Italy, Massalubrense, we lived in a small room, made of mud brick. Many people from my village come to New Zealand. My uncles, my brothers, finally my father, then my mother. And I am left in Massalubrense with my aunts, because the sea voyage is so long and I am so small. I am strong. I do the work of a boy. But then, when I am twelve years old, I must come to New Zealand. To a place where I cannot speak the language. To a family I do not know. And I hate this man who is my father! He is so cruel. And in my mother, I see a woman who is . . . so sad. And I feel myself, I am not like my sisters. I have the feelings of a boy. And every night, I pray to God I wake up a boy. And so I start to dress in my brother's clothes. I get a job on the West Coast. In the morning, I leave my father's house as a woman and on the way I change to a man. And only my brother knows this. Only then my brother, he takes me to meet his girlfriend. He introduce me as Jack. Only his girlfriend, she likes *me*. So my brother, he tells my father. And I am beaten. And beaten. But I cannot be anything else. So I must leave my father's house and I must keep dressing as a man. Until finally . . . I am a man.

Silence.

Violet: And your name? What is your name?

Pause.

Eugenia: My name is Eugenia.

Pause.

Violet: Eugenia.

Pause.

Eugenia: You said you would love me, whatever I had done.
Violet: Yes . . .
Eugenia: Then come with me. Come with me now.
Violet: And what! Live in constant fear? Fear that somebody will find out?
Eugenia: Nobody will find out.
Violet: But we'll always be afraid they will.
Eugenia: We'll go away from here.
Violet: I could not come with you, as man and wife . . . I could only come if . . .
Eugenia: If?
Violet: If you went as a woman.
Eugenia: Not possible.
Violet: Why not?
Eugenia: Not possible . . .
Violet: Think about it . . . People would think we were friends, they'd think we were sisters even. They'd never know anything about our private ways. Aye. That's the answer. That's the way we can be together. The way you can be yourself!
Eugenia, *horrified*: I do not know this self . . . this woman . . .
Violet: You can learn to know this self.

> Violet *talks beseechingly, amid desperate, small kisses, which she plants on* Eugenia's *face.*

Oh, Jack, Jack. Imagine. Imagine what it would mean. It

would mean we could love one another and no one would
ever know. No one could ever touch us, Jack!

EUGENIA, *pulling herself away*: I could not love you like that!

VIOLET: Why not? We do not have to be bound by custom, Jack!
Because the custom, in our case, is empty.

EUGENIA: I could not make love to you as a woman! That is
disgusting. I am not like that! You are not like that. We are
married. We are man and wife!

VIOLET: We are *not* man and wife, Eugenia! That is a lie against
nature.

EUGENIA: I do not know how you could be with me in that way.

VIOLET: I only know I cannot be with you in any other way.

EUGENIA: It is against my nature.

> *Pause.*

VIOLET: Then I cannot come with you.

EUGENIA: Oh God . . . God . . .

VIOLET: You'll have to go on your own. Tonight.

EUGENIA: Where should I go? I have nowhere.

VIOLET: You are a man. You can go anywhere.

EUGENIA: I cannot go without you.

VIOLET: If you stay, we must obtain an annulment.

EUGENIA: Then the whole town will know!

VIOLET: Do you not think the whole town will know already!

EUGENIA: I cannot let you do this! You must not do this!

VIOLET: If we cannot find a way that is right for us both, we must
go our separate ways.

EUGENIA: I would rather kill us both first!

VIOLET: Then kill yourself, Jack! It might give birth to something
real in the process!

> VIOLET *rushes out.* EUGENIA *paces frantically around. She
> is like a trapped animal, not knowing which way to turn.
> She puts on her jacket. She picks up the suitcase and opens
> it. She gets out the revolver. She is tormented, fearful. She
> slams the gun down on the table and leaves.* VIOLET *rushes
> in as* EUGENIA *leaves.*

VIOLET, *calling after her*: Jack! Jack!

VIOLET *paces aimlessly, realising with horror that* EUGENIA *has gone. She sees the gun and is shocked, fearful. She picks it up. The lights are switched off suddenly.* VIOLET *speaks in the darkness.*

Jack? Jack, what are you doing? Answer me. For goodness' sake, Jack, answer me! I know you're there and you'll not be frightening me, if that's what you're intending. I'm not afraid of the dark you know. Jack. Jack, answer me!

VIOLET *is grabbed from behind. A hand covers her mouth and she struggles and tries to speak. She tears the hand away and yells.*

Jack!

A gunshot is heard. There is the sound of flames, burning. WALLACE *enters in a pinpoint of light.*

WALLACE: Jack Martelli, you are arrested in connection with the murder of Violet Donovan.

WALLACE *exits.* GEORGINA *enters.*

Scene 5: Georgina's Office, the present

GEORGINA *is standing, looking dazed. She is holding the book that* IRIS *gave her earlier.* COOPER *rushes in.*

COOPER: Georgina! Lily Thompson is having hysterics in my office and the parents are going ballistic about this bloody play! They're on the way down here at this very moment. Now I don't know what's going on here, but I suggest you get that *Ms* Robinson of yours to sort this bloody mess out! And if you don't, then I will!

IRIS *rushes in.* COOPER *gives her a sharp look and leaves.*

IRIS: Look, I know there's a bit of drama happening around the play, but I just want to say that Lily is highly strung.

GEORGINA: Lily is having a nervous breakdown! And I'm starting to see things!

IRIS: *What?*
GEORGINA: Visions, nightmares, hallucinations!

   IRIS *scoffs.*

   Of her. Him. *Her!*
IRIS: It's your subconscious telling you to chill out.
GEORGINA: I don't know how you can treat this so lightly!
IRIS: I'm sorry, but I think you're letting them intimidate you.
GEORGINA: I think I'm letting you railroad me!
IRIS: What?
GEORGINA: I asked you to tone the piece down and you've
   completely ignored me!
IRIS: I've toned the bloody piece down so much it's starting to
   look like a washed out version of Cinderella! It's not the
   subject material that's dangerous, it's the terror of kids
   touching anything sexual. What do you think it's going to
   do to them? Turn them into a monstrous regiment of raving
   perverts!
GEORGINA: What makes you think you can just march in here
   and throw your liberal aspersions all over the place!
IRIS, *scofffing*: Liberal *aspersions!*
GEORGINA: And how dare you make assumptions about what I
   think!
IRIS: The only assumption I'm making is that this would make a
   challenging play. If it had half a chance. It's one of our stories!
GEORGINA: *Our* stories? Look, I'd like you to get something
   straight. I am not in the slightest bit like you! What happened
   between us two years ago, was a fly-by-night indiscretion! I
   am a respectable deputy principal, in a respectable indepen-
   dent school. Where I happen to be a respectable Head of
   English. A subject which I treat with the utmost . . . respect!
IRIS: Who are you trying to convince? Me or yourself?
GEORGINA: Look, I have a great deal of regard for your work, but
   I am no longer convinced that this is the time, or the place,
   for this particular parable to have its platform!
IRIS: Why are you seeing her?
GEORGINA: What?
IRIS: Why are you seeing Eugenia? Why is she showing herself?
   To you, in particular?

GEORGINA, *glaring at* IRIS: I have an overwhelming desire suddenly to sit in quiet contemplation. *If* you'll excuse me!

> IRIS *starts to leave then stops.*

IRIS: Is that how you unwind?

GEORGINA: Pardon?

IRIS: Why hasn't someone as attractive as you married again, Georgina?

GEORGINA: Men are put off by power-crazed women with crushing intellects who are no good at nurturing.

IRIS: Then perhaps you should find someone who doesn't need nurturing.

> *Pause.*

GEORGINA: Are you trying to seduce me?

> *Pause.* IRIS *is totally thrown off guard.*

IRIS: . . . Yes.

GEORGINA: Don't!

> IRIS *looks at her for a moment then exits.* GEORGINA *stays on, reading the book, throughout the following scene.*

Scene 6: Bassani's Boarding House, 1917

WALLACE *is questioning* RUBY. *It is obvious that these two know each other well. There is a sexual familiarity between them.*

WALLACE: Ruby Baker, are you trying to tell me, that the man we have arrested is in fact . . . a woman?

RUBY: I am tryin' to tell you that he is clipped in the clapper-stick!

WALLACE: You've had first-hand experience, have you?

RUBY: I've seen his whatsit! It comes on and off!

WALLACE: Can you tell me where you first met this fellow?

RUBY: Here. At Mrs Bassani's boarding house. I knew he was unusual right from the start. Soon as I saw him.

WALLACE: Unusual? In what way, unusual?

RUBY: Well, he treated me like a lady.

WALLACE: And you came to know him in the ah . . . biblical sense?

RUBY: Yeah. Only it wasn't very religious!

WALLACE: No. When you had relations with him, did you know that he was a she?

RUBY: Course not! I wouldn't have hit the pit with him if I'd known.

WALLACE: How did he treat you 'in the pit', Rube?

RUBY: He was lovely. He wasn't afraid to get his lips wet.

WALLACE: And when you found out his true nature, how did you feel?

RUBY: Ooh, I was disgusted!

WALLACE: So you wouldn't have had intimate relations with him after you found out?

RUBY: Well, I wouldn't say that exactly. Given half a chance, I might've!

WALLACE: Even though you knew he was a woman?

RUBY: Well, he wasn't like any woman I knew! Only that's what made him such a good kisser, see! 'Cause he was really a she, but when it come down to it, she knew she was meant to be a man, so in fact, she was really a he.

WALLACE: Would you call yourself a 'normal' woman?

RUBY: Course I'm normal! What are you driving at? How dare you!

WALLACE: So as soon as he married, your relations with him terminated?

RUBY: Yeah. Soon as he married, he only had eyes for Violet.

> RUBY *and* WALLACE *exit.*

> *The haunting notes of 'Bella Ciao' are heard, played slowly on a mandolin.* VIOLET *rushes in. It is as if she is searching for someone. She sees* GEORGINA *and stops.* GEORGINA *looks up from her book and stares at her.* VIOLET *walks slowly over to* GEORGINA *and touches her face. The touch of a lover.* GEORGINA *is transfixed.* VIOLET *exits. Then* GEORGINA *exits.*

Scene 7: Back Yard,
Bassani's Boarding House, 1917

MRS BASSANI *enters with a basket which she collects wood in.*
WALLACE *is taking a statement from her.*

MRS BASSANI: Sì, Detective Wallace, after he married, he had eyes only for Violetta.

WALLACE: Mrs Bassani, when did you start to suspect that Jack was really a Jill?

MRS BASSANI: After we had spent some nights together.

WALLACE: What made you realise this?

MRS BASSANI: I gave him my husband's razor. He did not touch it.

WALLACE: Surely, Mrs Bassani, this would not give you ample cause to suspect a man was really a woman. Else one might suspect the less hirsute members of our sex! *He chuckles.*

MRS BASSANI: No, no. There were . . . other things.

WALLACE: Would you care to tell me what these 'other things' were?

MRS BASSANI, *embarrassed*: I do not like to . . . The first night we were together, we made love for many hours. Non stop.

WALLACE, *clearing his throat, embarrassed*: And suspecting this, you still continued to have carnal relations with him?

MRS BASSANI: Sì. She was the best man I ever know!

MRS BASSANI *exits. Lighting change.*

Scene 8: Police Station, 1917

EUGENIA *enters.*

EUGENIA: I do not want to be lined up like a criminal! I have done nothing!

WALLACE: Have you got any distinguishing marks on your body which might help us to prove your identity?

EUGENIA: No! I do not!

WALLACE: Strip off a little then and let's have a look at you.

EUGENIA: No! I will not do that!

WALLACE: Have you got something to hide, Jack?

EUGENIA: No.

WALLACE: We've got reason to believe you're not all you appear to be.

EUGENIA: What do you mean?

WALLACE: We've got a little problem, Jack. We're not sure what cell to put you in. The men's or the women's.

EUGENIA: But I am a man.

WALLACE: Course you are and I'm Queen Victoria! Shall I just show you what I found in your suitcase?

> WALLACE *opens the suitcase, takes out a small wooden box and opens it.*

What's this, Jack?

EUGENIA: Something . . .

WALLACE: Something artificial? Something you've been using?

EUGENIA: Something I needed . . . for my wife.

WALLACE: So this simulacrum, 'Jack', is what you might call your manhood!

EUGENIA: I did not want my wife to find out.

WALLACE: What, you mean to say she didn't know, even after you were married?

> *Pause.*

EUGENIA: No. She did not know for sure . . . until last night.

WALLACE: You are a very confused young woman, 'Jack'. You have cultivated a patina of lies to hide your true sex. That is, if you know anymore what your true sex is! And this crude carnal counterfeit is the grotesque symbol of your sick longings!

EUGENIA: No, no . . . I was in love with my wife . . . my wife . . . I was in love with my . . . my . . .

> *Lighting change.* IRIS *appears. She carries a ghetto blaster.*

Scene 9: School Hall, the present

IRIS *starts choreographing some dance steps to the music of K.D. Lang's version of Cole Porter's 'So In Love With You Am I'. Her mind is elsewhere, but she eventually gets carried away with the dance which has a sensual and sad feel to it.* GEORGINA *enters, unseen by* IRIS, *and watches her. After a moment* IRIS *sees her and stops. She turns off the music.*

GEORGINA: Mozart. I like Mozart.

> *Pause.*

That's how I unwind.

> *Pause.*

'Ave Verum Corpus' is a particular favourite.
IRIS: I've always enjoyed Mozart.

> *Pause.*

GEORGINA: She was innocent.

> *Pause.*

Eugenia was innocent.

> *Pause.*

IRIS: Violet died from a bullet wound from Eugenia's gun for Chrissake.
GEORGINA: Which doesn't mean she pulled the trigger!
IRIS: They didn't lock her up for not shaving her legs.
GEORGINA, *fervently*: Didn't they? Her sexual conduct alone would've ensured she be locked up.
IRIS: She obviously panicked. I can relate to that. She was freaked.
GEORGINA: Not freaked. *A* freak! Think about it.

> *Pause.*

IRIS: You think she was framed?
GEORGINA: I think she was framed.
IRIS: Why shouldn't she be a bad girl? Why shouldn't she be a rotten bugger? Rotten to the core! That's what makes her

fascinating. Women do kill occasionally. Why sanitise her story just because she was a lesbian?

> COOPER *enters and addresses* GEORGINA.

COOPER: I need to see you immediately!
GEORGINA, *barely looking at him*: Two minutes.

> COOPER *stands listening to the two women.* GEORGINA *continues to talk to* IRIS, *in full flight.*

GEORGINA: Who says she was a lesbian?
IRIS: It's obvious!
GEORGINA: Where is it obvious? She saw herself as a heterosexual man. A transsexual, at most. She didn't admit to being a lesbian!
IRIS, *eyeballing her*: A lot of women don't.

> COOPER *exits.*

GEORGINA, *flustered*: She didn't identify that way. She obviously couldn't admit to . . . her position was such that . . .
IRIS: What position?
GEORGINA: What I mean is, the times were such that she . . . she . . .
IRIS: She couldn't quite open that closet door.

> *Pause.*

GEORGINA: Exactly!

> *Pause.*

IRIS: So, what do you want me to do about it? Get her a royal pardon?
GEORGINA: Why not!
IRIS: Not a problem! Anything else?
GEORGINA: Yes. Rewrite it!
IRIS: What?
GEORGINA: Oscar Wilde once said, 'The one duty we owe to history, is to rewrite it!'
IRIS: Oscar Wilde was a queer.

> *Pause.*

GEORGINA: Indeed. I copied this poem. It was in Violet's book. *She hands* IRIS *a copy of the poem.* Include it.

> *They hold each other's look for a second then* GEORGINA *leaves.* IRIS *is a little bemused. She looks at the poem and starts to read it.*

IRIS: 'I like to say your name. I like the lilt of it on my lips. I like the way it slips and . . .

> IRIS *is taken aback. The poem is hauntingly familiar, yet she does not know why. There is a subtle lighting change. She continues to read aloud.*

'. . . I like the way it slips and slides, as I test and try. I like the way it captures your essence. I like its poem, and rhyme. Its cadent candescence, its peak and its prime. And most of all, I like the way I can take it and tone it. Any time of night or day. Your taste on my lips.'

> IRIS *sits, totally bemused, pondering the words of the poem. She stays on throughout the following two scenes, totally in her own world.*

Scene 10: Georgina's Office, the present

COOPER *and* GEORGINA *enter.*

COOPER: I don't give a toss whether she's innocent! I cannot see that this is a remotely palatable subject for a college student! That bloody drama teacher of yours wants her head read! Georgina, we are a business. Not a bloody freak show! A cheap-rate circus. With a bearded bloody woman out the back!

GEORGINA: Cooper, this woman was guilty before she was even tried! She was hounded by fear. It is only by looking at that fear that any of us can ever hope to comprehend what drives a woman to live like this! *That* is what the students will learn from it!

COOPER: Georgina, this piece is creating a tidal wave and it's threatening to come crashing down on our heads! Ditch it!

If you've got any sense of survival, send it packing. *He starts to leave.*

GEORGINA, *calling desperately after him*: Eugenia left the confectionery shop at 11 p.m. She was found at the Bassani household at 11.30 p.m. Half an hour later! Half an hour is the exact time it takes to walk there. Briskly. I've timed it. It would've given her just enough time to get there, sit down and pour herself a stiff drink! Now if . . .

COOPER: Why are you doing this?

GEORGINA, *groping for an answer*: To set the record straight. We can at least present her in this play as innocent!

COOPER: Georgina, if we lose students over this, someone's head's going to roll!

GEORGINA: But I think I can prove it!

COOPER: Georgina! What the crap does it matter? *He starts to go.*

GEORGINA, *calling after him*: She was in love with her for Chrissake! She was hardly likely to kill the woman she loved . . . She was . . . She was . . .

COOPER: She was an offender against God's gift of gender!

> COOPER exits. GEORGINA *is holding back tears—only just. She exits.*

Scene 11: School Hall, the present

IRIS *is still in her own world, the poem in her hand.* VIC *enters. She dances the steps that* IRIS *was choreographing earlier. She's wearing a half-male, half-female costume. She dances to the music of 'So In Love With You Am I'. The dance has a slightly surreal feel to it. She and* IRIS *are unaware of each other. The dance ends and* VIC *exits.* IRIS *picks up the ghetto blaster and, still engrossed in the poem, exits.*

Scene 12: Police Station, 1917

WALLACE: Jack Martelli! We don't even know if you're a man or a woman! So how can we believe a word that comes out of your cunning little kisser!

EUGENIA: I do not know who killed my wife!

WALLACE: Your neighbour heard your gun go off! And saw you walking up the street with a suitcase! You shot your poor Violet. Then you sniffed around to Signora Bassani's house, to give yourself an alibi! Isn't that so! Answer me, you polluted little pervert!

EUGENIA: I am innocent. On the night of the terrible . . . the terrible . . . On the night. Vincent, he came to our house. He abused me in front of my wife! When he left, we had . . . we had words. Then I leave. I walk, I walk. I walk to Signora Bassani's.

Lighting change.

Scene 13: Mrs Bassani's Kitchen, 1916

Flashback. The night of the murder.

EUGENIA *is sitting at the table with a bottle of whisky and a glass in front of her. She is quite drunk.* MRS BASSANI *enters, singing 'Auld Lang Syne'. She is surprised and delighted to see* EUGENIA.

MRS BASSANI: Ciao, Jack! Così bello di vederti! Mo' mi sento tanto la tua mancanza. (*It is so good to see you! I have missed you too much.*) It is not even midnight yet! Why are you not celebrating the new year with Violetta?

EUGENIA: She does not want me anymore. Mi anno detto di lasciarti. (*She told me to go away.*) She told me to go away.

MRS BASSANI: Then tonight you stay with me! Tomorrow, in the morning, everything looks different.

EUGENIA: She is wanting a divorce, Rosa.

MRS BASSANI: Sì, Violetta, she is a strange woman. First she is not liking the men, then she is marrying one. Mamma mia! The Irish!

EUGENIA: Tu non capisci. Tu non capisci. (*You don't understand.*) She want me to be different. Different.

MRS BASSANI: Jack. Look at me. You *are* different. What does she want? What?

EUGENIA: She wants I am a different person.

MRS BASSANI: Ah! Is better for the woman to change. Not the man.

EUGENIA: . . . the woman, the woman . . .

MRS BASSANI: Sì sì, is life. Because the woman, she is strong. Because she has the bambino. She has the agony of the birth of the bambino. Ah! The man, he would faint at the thought! The men are so weak. But we let them think they are strong. Because God is a man. And we cannot have a God who thinks he is a coward!

EUGENIA: For me to change . . . is like turning the swan back into the ugly duckling.

MRS BASSANI: What is ugly to you is bello to her.

EUGENIA: Sì . . . maybe . . . *She takes a swig of whisky.* Then maybe I must kill myself first!

MRS BASSANI: Ah! You have drunk too much. You talk stupid. Come, I put you to bed. I put you in my bed.

EUGENIA: No. No, Rosa. I must find the duck pond. The little pond. And maybe I float, or maybe I drown. But . . . Maybe she teach me to swim. *She struggles drunkenly to her feet and chuckles.* As a very ugly duckling!

> EUGENIA *stumbles out.*

MRS BASSANI, *calling after her*: Jack! If she not like the quack, you come back to Rosa's nest, sì?

> MRS BASSANI *exits. Lighting change back.*

Scene 14: Police Station, 1917

EUGENIA: And so I think to myself, I will tell my wife, I will tell her that I can be strong. So I leave Signora Bassani. And I run back to tell her. I run. And I run. But then I see that the shop is on fire! And the fire is all flames! And I run. And I fall. And the smoke is in the air. And I cannot cry out. Because my heart is on fire! And Violet, she is . . . she is lying . . .

> WALLACE *physically harasses* EUGENIA *throughout the following. She starts to break down.*

WALLACE: Lying on the floor where you left her!

EUGENIA: No . . .

WALLACE: Before you left the house!

EUGENIA: No. When I left her, she was alive!

WALLACE: You killed her!

EUGENIA: No!

WALLACE: Then you returned to the scene of the disgusting deed and you set fire to the evidence!

EUGENIA: No! I was going to tell her we could be happy.

WALLACE: Then why did you tell Mrs Bassani you must kill yourself?

EUGENIA: Because in my body, I am a woman. I meant to kill a . . . [part of myself.]

WALLACE: In your body you are a barbarian! And you meant to kill an innocent woman!

EUGENIA: This is not true.

WALLACE: Your gun was found next to the body! Cartridges were found in your suitcase!

EUGENIA: I left my gun . . .

WALLACE: You're an invert, Jack! A filthy little female-husband! A malformation! You killed the woman you married, because she wouldn't keep your dirty little secret!

EUGENIA: No. This is false! I did not kill my wife. I did nothing wrong. I am not guilty!

WALLACE: Tell that to the judge!

> WALLACE *exits.*

EUGENIA, *shouting*: Io non ho fatto questo! Sono innocente! Innocente! Non lo so chi è stato. Non ho mai toccata a lei. Sono innocente! (*I did not do this! I am innocent! Innocent! I do not know who did this. I would never have hurt her. I am innocent!*) *She talks through sobs.* I left her. I left her, after we argued. I should have gone back. I heard her calling my name . . . but I kept walking . . . I should have gone back . . . But I kept walking . . . Walking . . .

> *Blackout.*

Scene 15: Violet's Flower Shop, 1917

Flashback.

Violet *screams in the darkness.*

Violet: Jack!

> *A match is struck and* Vincent *is standing over* Violet. *He puts the gun next to* Violet*'s body. He throws the lighted match onto the ground. Blackout.* Vincent *exits. The raging sound of flames is heard. There is smoke and the flicker of fire.* Eugenia *rushes in and sees* Violet.

Eugenia: Violet! Violet!

> Eugenia *rushes to* Violet *and kneels beside her. She holds her in her arms and tries to rouse her.*

Parla con me. Parla con me! Chi ha fatto quello a te. (*Speak to me. Who has done this to you.*) Parla con me. Who has done this to you? Parla con me!

> Eugenia *rocks* Violet *like a baby—talking to her, trying to bring her back to life, even though she knows it is too late.*

No, it is not possible! Speak to me! Ho cambiato pensiero. (*I have changed my mind.*) Non è troppo tardi. (*It is not too late.*) It is not too late. We can go away! Speak to me. I am a woman! Io sono donna. Io non sono più uomo. (*I am a woman. I am no longer a man.*) E tutto è passato. (*All that is past.*) I am a woman now. It is not too late. I will change. I am a woman. A woman. *She screams out the words.* I am a woman!

> *A mournful Italian folksong is heard.* Vic, Murray *and* Lily *enter dancing a traditional funereal step. They are like surreal figures. They lift* Violet *and put her in* Eugenia*'s arms. The flames crackle fiercely over faces and bodies.* Eugenia *carries* Violet *off. The dancers continue their dance. At the end of the dance,* Murray *steps forward.*

Murray (Wallace): Eugenia Maria Martelli, you have been found guilty of the murder of Violet Donovan. You are sentenced to death by hanging.

> GEORGINA *appears in a pinpoint of light just before the end of* WALLACE'S *statement. It is almost as if he is saying it to her, yet neither is aware of the other.*

Scene 16: School Hall, the present

GEORGINA *is sitting quietly.* COOPER *enters. Pause.*

COOPER: The play is a dead duck, Georgina. The Board want it axed.

> *Pause.*

GEORGINA: Oh.

COOPER: Look, I know this is play is important to you. But if you don't can the frigging thing fast, you'll be dusting blackboards in the year 2000.

GEORGINA: Why does that sound like blackmail?

COOPER: Because it is. Because Lily's parents are transferring Lily to another school. Because when you're trying to attract a bigger roll, that's not a good look.

GEORGINA: What do they want? A principal or a bloody profit manager? The kids will be devastated!

COOPER: They'll get over it.

GEORGINA: Victoria Stevens got herself suspended twice last year! Doing the play has transformed her.

COOPER, *scoffing*: Into what?

> *Pause.*

GEORGINA: And if I don't comply?

> *Pause.*

COOPER: You'll be asked to resign.

GEORGINA: Christ . . . *She has the wind taken out of her sails.*

> *Pause.*

COOPER: Now get yourself together. The Board want an audience with you in ten minutes.

GEORGINA: Jesus.

>COOPER *exits.* IRIS *comes rushing in.*

IRIS: I've rewritten the beginning. It now starts with a dance. Have you got a moment? Can I show you the dance?

GEORGINA: There isn't going to be a show.

>*Pause.*

IRIS: What?

GEORGINA: The Board have canned it. I'm sorry . . .

IRIS: Isn't there anything we can do?

GEORGINA: It's a fait accompli.

IRIS: We'll put it on somewhere else then! The students are all seventh formers, they're all leaving in four months. We'll do it as a Christmas production!

GEORGINA: Oh yes. Let's do it as a nativity play!

>IRIS *looks at her, not knowing whether she is joking or not.*

We could throw in a few shepherds. Bung in the odd bit of straw. We'll get the board to sell ice creams in the interval. Fling flowers on the opening night.

>IRIS *is devastated.*

We'd piss them off so much, we'd be lucky to teach kindergarten in Kathmandu after that!

IRIS: Christ! Bastards! *She sits.*

>*Pause.*

GEORGINA: Maybe Eugenia didn't need us to do the play. Maybe she just needed us to know that she was innocent.

>*Pause.*

IRIS, *looking at her in surprise*: You're a strange mix.

>*Pause.*

GEORGINA, *smiling, in an Italian accent*: I see two sides of the same coin.

IRIS *looks at her with a vague sense of déjà vu.*

IRIS: Well, that must be very . . . perplexing for you.

GEORGINA: No. Is good.

Pause.

IRIS, *looking lost*: I don't know what to do . . .

Pause.

GEORGINA, *gently*: Show me the dance.

> IRIS *stands, not taking her eyes off* GEORGINA. *Three or four solo notes of 'Bella Ciao' are heard. The two women face one another as the lights fade to a tight spot on* GEORGINA. IRIS *exits.*

GEORGINA: I realise I have stepped out of line. I would like the Board to accept my apology. In my defence, I believed I was viewing the larger picture. The picture of justice. But what I was seeing was the smaller picture. The picture of fear. I understand now how fear drives us. I myself have always feared a mediocrity of imagination—the death of creativity. Into our creativity is poured knowledge. It is a great gift. A gift which we all possess. All fear is connected with death. The fear to leap: to fall to one's death. The fear to be what we truly are: the death of an old self-image . . .

> *Three or four notes of the mandolin are heard.* VIOLET *runs on. It is as though she is looking for* EUGENIA. GEORGINA *and* VIOLET *look at each other.* GEORGINA *pauses.*

I'm sorry . . . I'm sorry but I cannot accept this position of principal.

> GEORGINA *exits.*

VIOLET, *calling after* GEORGINA. *It is as though she is calling* EUGENIA *to her, conjuring her up*: Do you remember when the moonlight came creeping in through our window, Jack? Do you remember its light falling on our kisses? How it came in night after night, whether we invited it or not. It was a rude, crude moon, Jack. Do you remember how it would take off over the hills, as it climbed in flight? Like a bird at its height. And while the world was asleep, how we'd follow it. Swallow it, whole. And then in the morning how it would dim on the rim of the horizon. How its pale face would fade, as our thoughts strayed into a sleepy day. Another lifetime away. The moon's setting now, Jack. It's setting. It's just a thin shape in the sky. It's making way for the dawn.

> *Three or four solo notes of the mandolin are heard.* EUGENIA *enters dressed in her suit and hat. She and* VIOLET *speak directly to each other.*

EUGENIA: Sometimes now, when I am remembering that life, my thoughts fade into yesterday and I am afloat in that other world. So close now, it seems, that I wonder if it was this life or another life, or something I once dreamed. And then I see your face. Your eyes. And the picture of a small flower shop, in a small suburb, where the shelves are lined with tobacco, with candy and where uncut flowers lie unwrapped on a small wooden table . . .

VIOLET: Do you believe we live again and again, Jack?

EUGENIA: The spirit is old. So old . . . Older than the trees, the moon, the sands . . .

VIOLET: Do you believe we live again?

EUGENIA: And then I return from our world . . . and I remember, I am a woman now. And not a man.

> EUGENIA *removes her hat. The music to 'Bella Ciao' floats in.* VIOLET *and* EUGENIA *stay looking at each other. The other characters enter, singing 'Bella Ciao'. They are dressed in their 1916 costumes. The entire cast dances the tarantella for the last two verses of the song.*

Bella Ciao
Traditional